Shaping the Next

Generation

Shaping the Next } Generation

Helping Parents Seize Their Brief Window of Opportunity

David & Elaine Atchison

THOMAS NELSON PUBLISHERS®
Nashville

Published in Nashville, Tennessee, by Thomas Nelson, Inc.

Scripture quotations noted NKJV are from THE NEW KING JAMES VERSION.
Copyright © 1979, 1980, 1982, Thomas Nelson, Inc., Publishers.

Scripture quotations noted NIV are from the HOLY BIBLE: NEW INTERNA-
TIONAL VERSION®. Copyright © 1973, 1978, 1984 by International Bible
Society. Used by permission of Zondervan Publishing House. All rights
reserved.

Scripture quotations noted NASB are from the NEW AMERICAN STANDARD
BIBLE (R), © Copyright The Lockman Foundation 1960, 1962, 1963, 1968,
1971, 1972, 1973, 1975, 1977. Used by permission.

Scripture quotations noted CEV are from THE CONTEMPORARY ENGLISH
VERSION. © 1991 by the American Bible Society. Used by permission.

Scripture quotations noted The Message are from *The Message: The New
Testament in Contemporary English.* Copyright © 1993 by Eugene H. Peterson.

ISBN 0-7852-6968-1

Published in the United States of America

1 2 3 4 5 6 QPV 04 03 02 01 00 99

Dedicated to David Blake, Joel Matthew, and Amanda Brooke

*You fill our lives,
challenge our wits,
keep us humble,
and inspire our dreams for the future.*

*Love,
Mom and Paps*

Contents

Acknowledgments

Our Heavenly Father, for the hope of His calling;

Our earthly parents—alias, Gran and Gramps, Gammy and Papa—for loving us "through it all;"

Mark and Susan Scott, faithful friends, who believed in us when we were still unsure of God's plans;

Ray Moss, who first asked us to deveolp a Bible Study for young parents—and Bob and Cindy Landham, who carried the torch by teaching it for so many years;

The Hobbs, Austs, Seals, and O'Shoneys, and all the other moms and dads who really took the parenting principles to heart—it's all our fault!

Billy Beacham and Student Discipleship Ministries, who first gave us the opportunity to spread our wings and develop *Shaping* as a transferable resource;

Fred Carpenter, who planted the seed that our scribblings could become something more;

John Kramp, who blazed the trail and guided us to many open doors;

Lee Sizemore, Jimmy Hester, and our LifeWay friends, who taught us to dream in video;

Mike Hyatt and Cindy Blades, our patient editors at Thomas Nelson Publishers, who kindly answered our constant questions, and held our hands through the entire process;

Our pastor, Scott Patty, our Grace Community family, and the "Southside group" for loving us so well;

Our grandparents—the Atchisons, Winternheimers, Everetts, and Stallworths—who quietly shaped the next generation and the spiritual heritage we enjoy today.

Introduction

It's great living in the perfect family . . .Your wife not only keeps the house in order and kids under control, but she is always in a great mood and has the time and energy to give you her undivided attention in the evenings. When you've had an extra hard day, she gives you back rubs and foot massages after the children are in bed . . .

It's great living in the perfect family . . . Your husband divides all of the household and parenting duties right down the middle. He bathes the kids, does the laundry, drives on field trips, and finds a sitter for your weekly dates. Oh—and at least twice a year he says, "Honey, you and a friend need to get away for a few days of rest at the beach."

Not only that, the children are always eager to please Mom and Dad and they are so respectful!

When the household jobs are assigned, they say, "Happy to do it, Mom," and always ask Dad, "What can I do to make your life easier?"

Amazingly, the children don't fight and squabble. Instead, they build each other up and are always willing to share their clothes and CDs. The neighbors always comment that they've never known better-behaved children and the principal only calls when it's time to give out awards.

Meal times are special, too, because everyone lingers at the table to discuss the affairs of the day, and the practical spiritual insights they are learning. But the icing on the cake is that even after twelve hours in the car, no one cries, "Are we there yet?" or "She touched me!"

Isn't it great living in the perfect family?

We can only imagine, because our household rarely resembles the image we just fabricated!

In reality, we are like other families who love God and each other, yet struggle daily with issues like breakdowns in communication, self-centeredness that leads to conflict, and chaotic schedules that compete with relationship building. Meal times are important in the Atchison household, but there is very little lingering there.

We are blessed to have three active teenagers, who, by God's grace, are growing in their Christian faith and obey pretty well for adolescents. We have to admit that they work hard around the house. (If you ever saw the movie *Three Men and a Baby,* at our house it's *Three Slaves and a Lady*). However, they are certainly not above voicing their disapproval at our decisions, sibling conflict is alive and well, and we have had more than one call from the principal that had nothing to do with awards!

The bottom line is, *we aren't the perfect family.* In fact, one of the kids recently said they wondered if they would still want us to write a book if someone came and videtaped our family! That brings up a question that an acquaintance from our children's school brought up: "What gives you the right to tell other parents how to raise their children?" Good question.

Let's be very clear on the front end—we do not consider ourselves experts on parenting. It seems that the only experts on parenting are those who have never had children. The rest of us are far too vulnerable to make such a claim. Before we ever had children, we were concerned about what kind of parents we would be—and what God expects from parents who are followers of Christ. Believing that *"His divine power has given us everything we need for life and godliness" (2 Peter 1:3),* we began to explore what the Bible has to say about children and parents. Despite the fact that we live in a cynical culture that has lost it moral compass and confidence in the family, God began to stir and inspire us. He has provided *every* mother and father with the necessary equipment to love, train, and prepare their children to become leaders within their generation.

Therefore, we consider ourselves fellow learners with you—traveling the same awesome journey called parenthood. Over the last decade of researching, teaching, and writing on the subject of parenting, we have become more convinced—and more convicted—that God offers vision, hope, and help for any parent who will seize their brief window of opportunity to shape the next generation.

David and Elaine Atchison

Part One:

Correcting Your Vision

Blindness may be caused by anything that prevents light from reaching the optic nerve of the eye or the part of the brain connected with vision. Not many people are born blind, but many lose their sight from preventable causes. Louis Braille adapted a coded system for blind people, using groups of one to six raised dots. This system is now used by visually impaired persons throughout the English-speaking world and is used in most other languages, including Chinese. Helen Keller was born in 1880, and at nineteen months old, she suffered an acute illness that left her deaf and blind. She could not be educated until the age of seven when Anne Sullivan began to teach her to read by the Braille system and to write by means of a special typewriter. At age ten, Keller learned to speak after only one month of study. Ten years later, she was able to enter Radcliffe College, where she graduated with honors and went on to be an inspiration to others. Helen Keller was once asked if there is anything worse than being blind. She answered, "Yes. Being able to see, but having no vision." Everyone enters parenthood with unique hopes and dreams for their child. We all wear unique "lenses" prescribed by family background, past experiences, and differing worldviews. We all need fresh optimism and vision for the next generation. And we need it now—for children won't wait! Expanding our vision for the next generation begins with a new vision of God. In God's economy, vision is not reserved for the rich, the strong, or the brilliant. God often chooses ordinary people to demonstrate *extraordinary* vision! On November 19, 1997 Kenny and Bobbi McCaughey's lives changed forever. Bobbi made medical history by giving birth to the world's first surviving septuplets. Initially, the doctors recommended "selective reduction" (aborting one or more fetuses) because of the high risk of mortality and health problems for multiple, premature babies. The McCaugheys understood the dangers, yet chose to trust the Giver of life—the One who said, "Children are a gift from God." Today, all seven children are thriving, and the world has witnessed them giving God all the glory! The next four chapters will serve as an eye exam revealing your attitudes and perceptions on parenthood. Ask the heavenly Father to correct and expand your vision before you embark on the journey of shaping the next generation.

1 ⟩ Precious in His Sight

*"The counsel of the LORD stands forever,
The plans of His heart to all generations."*
—Psalm 33:11 NKJV

At last, he was asleep! I wasn't sure what time it was—between 2:00 and 4:00 A.M.—it doesn't make much difference. Blake was nestled securely on my chest as my grandmother's rocking chair continued its familiar creaking. I didn't hear Joel crying, so I figured Elaine was already sleeping. I was accustomed to the inner debate that followed. Who was to blame for not getting enough sleep? I should feel grateful and proud to be the father of identical twin sons. I was proud, but I was exhausted from the grueling routine of an "involved father." I needed to be strong for Elaine—beginning motherhood with two at once is tough, but how could I keep up this pace? Didn't anyone care that I was in the middle of my first real estate development?

As I kept rocking, more ominous thoughts pushed their way into my mind. *What in the world am I doing as a father? What if I can't support the family—a mortgage, double diapers . . . double college tuition! Forget college, how will Blake and Joel make it through high school?* We were youth leaders in our church and knew all too well the struggles even "good" kids battle. We had recently completed some research on the New Age movement and I reviewed the deceptions our children would face. By now, a sense of acute anxiety coursed through my entire being while Blake slept peacefully—ready to be put in his crib so I could finally get some rest. But I just kept rocking. I had to hold him a little longer. This father thing was definitely getting to me.

Halfway around the world, another mother and father weren't sleeping, either. They were seasoned parents, but related firsthand to our earliest parental concerns. They already had an older son and daughter, but their baby boy had quickly become the apple of their eye. When they looked into his distinct, dark eyes, they wondered who he might grow up to be. However, times had changed for the worse, and their government was legislating the right to bear children. They had surpassed their quota and were faced with the threat of infanticide. We can hardly relate to a culture that literally snatches children from their parents, but that is what Amram and Jochebed were facing three millennia ago. From the moment of his birth, there appeared in Moses something extraordinary, but their options were running out. They must have held little Moses close, the way I was holding Blake that night. But God had an unseen plan. Just at the time when Pharaoh's cruelty reached its height, He sent His deliverer into that generation. Moses' faithful parents are pointed out in the Hebrews "Hall of Faith" as parents who recognized God's vision for their child. They took great risks to protect him at any cost. "By faith Moses' parents hid him for three months after he was born, because they saw he was no ordinary child, and they were not afraid of the king's edict" (Heb. 11:23, NIV). When they couldn't hide him any longer, they devised a plan for his rescue. When they finally released him to God's protection, God Himself took over, orchestrating for Moses to grow up in an Egyptian palace while remaining under his mother's care for the next few years.

An Anxious Generation

We may not live in a time as threatening as Moses, yet *vague anxiety* exemplifies contemporary parents. It took one of our neighbors a year to allow her daughter to play inside our house. Two years later, she still walked her daughter over, then returned for her when the girls were finished playing. Why are parents so suspicious—even paranoid? Increasing reports of schoolyard violence in towns representing small-town America haven't helped. At any given moment, several nagging questions occupy our minds.

What If My Worst Nightmares Come True?

Elaine grew up in one of the nation's largest cities, so we wanted to find a smaller, safer place to rear our three children. The first time we drove into the square of historic Franklin, Tennessee and saw two young boys riding their bikes around the Civil War monument at dusk, we knew that's how we wanted our kids to grow up! That was twelve years ago. One afternoon last summer, an armed robber entered a church in our community, wounding an employee before eluding police helicopters and search dogs. Meanwhile, our boys were swimming one block away and our daughter, Amanda, was attending a day camp at another church down the street. *Another* reminder that there are no guarantees—anywhere. Even within well-groomed, closed-gated communities, one hears horrifying stories from abductions to abuse that make the imagination run wild. Most of us are like a Ping-Pong ball bouncing between dread and denial that such things could ever happen to us.

Am I Doing Enough for My Children?

Time magazine attempted to profile the deeper forces at work behind the rise of school shootings. "Were they simply bad seeds, genetic and spiritual misfits born without the brain chemistry that produces compassion—and indeed without souls? Or was nurture to blame? Is America's gun culture at fault? Or did the kids kill because they were molested by perverts, beaten by parents, rejected by girlfriends, despised by classmates or revved up by 'role playing games, heavy metal music, violent cartoons/TV and sugared cereal . . .'?"[1] As we approach a new millennium, the hazards of raising children have radically multiplied. At least that's how the media report it. The final finger always seems to point to dazed parents who never saw it coming.

What If My Kids Don't Turn Out Right?

Parents hate hearing nightmare statistics about teenagers. We used to comfort ourselves thinking, *Those aren't our kids.* Josh McDowell and Bob Hostetler blew our theory when they wrote *Right from Wrong.* Partnering with George Barna, they surveyed more than 3,700 active, churchgoing students from eleven to eighteen years old, who perfectly fit the profile of "our kids." In the end, their life-style choices were virtually no different from those of unchurched teens in our country. For example:

1 in 6 measured right vs. wrong by whether it works.
1 in 8 accepted breaking the law if it doesn't harm others.
Almost 1 in 5 eleven- and twelve-year-olds believed it is always or sometimes okay to have sex.[2]

Their strong message gave us a new sense of urgency about the need for intentional character building before middle school—but what do we mean by *turning out right?* Can parents *turn out* children like muffins from a pan? Will they turn out *right* only if we use the correct recipe and ingredients? That leads to another haunting question.

Can I Really Influence My Children?

A denominational newsletter reported that 75 percent of

Americans believe that parents have less influence on their children than schools, media, or government. Tragically, parents are buying into the myth that there is little, if anything, we can do to influence the lives of our own children—much less an entire generation. Historically, parents consulted their extended families for wisdom and support. The breakdown of families and our mobile society have caused more parents to seek outside resources for help in child rearing. The trend is to allow daycare, schools, and even churches to assume the primary role in shaping the child. Television and radio provide continuous programming for parents. Innumerable magazines and books are readily available—there's even the World Wide Web of interactive parental expertise! But how can parents know whom to trust?

THE CULTURAL LENS

Our daughter, Amanda, recently made the transition from glasses to contact lenses. Surprisingly, she failed the vision test, even with her glasses on. Over time, her eyesight completely changed—and she didn't even realize it. Our approach to parenting is determined by the "lenses" through which we view children. Parents may unwittingly adopt a "cultural lens" that limits and distorts vision. Like a pocket camera, it draws attention only to a small area, and what appears on the surface. Through a cultural lens, children appear to be unnecessary inconveniences, risks and liabilities. Besides the obvious financial risks, children are considered educational, behavioral, and vocational risks as well.

Our generation has been a trendsetter, pushing the envelope on the definition of "family." Even though we have witnessed a determined effort to reclaim strong family values, there is still a large gap between cultural and biblical views on the importance of family. In some circles, a couple have to go against the opinions of friends and coworkers to have children. *Maybe One,* by Bill McKibben, encourages parents to restrict their family to one child to protect against the environmental and emotional descent of man in coming generations.[3] Couples who do have children feel urgency for them to grow up, because child rearing often conflicts with careers. In *The Hurried Child,* David Elkind wrote that the idea that children can be hurried when they are young is a rationalization for parents "who love their children but . . . have neither the time nor the energy for childhood."[4] Another interesting commentary comes from the Church Growth Institute's seminar, "How to Reach the Baby Boomer" (the generation born between 1945 and 1964). The adolescent period of Depression Children (born 1925–45) lasted only four years. The baby boomer's adolescence lasted an average of *eight* years. The baby busters (born 1965–85) have shown a pattern of extending the adolescent period as long as *sixteen* years.[5] In other words, the generation that has been most hurried to grow up is taking longer than ever to leave the nest!

Cultural Currency

Over two decades ago, James Dobson wrote *Hide or Seek,* warning parents about conditional acceptance, which communicates "I love you when . . ." or "I love you if . . ." He described the Bank of Human Worth—an institution where three forms of currency are exchanged for love. The gold coin of beauty. The silver coin of achievement. The bronze coin of possessions.[6] All of us are appraised by this standard in our schools, careers, and communities. You may have grown up in a home where "good" performance was exchanged for acceptance. Most of us would be ashamed if we realized how many transactions we make every day at the Bank of Human Worth. Such a distorted focus leads to an overemphasis on *performance building.* Our energy and money and time become geared toward building up—or fixing up the child. The competition between parents wanting their child to stand out—or at least fit in—can be fierce, while the helpless child complies, hoping to please her anxious parents. If we continue to wear a cultural lens, we will lose sight of all God has designed our children to become. We will merely "hope for the best" as we struggle to survive parenthood.

THE BIBLICAL LENS

Amanda's doctor designed a lens requiring several adjustments before she could see perfectly. She learned how to insert and remove the lenses, and gradually wore them for longer periods of time. After a few days, she was hooked, and would never consider going back to the old lenses. God provides a different lens through which to view our children. This "biblical lens" is more like a telescope—revealing more than the naked eye can perceive. A biblical lens uncovers the "inner person," which cannot be identified by DNA or chromosome studies. Self-worth is determined according to God's economy rather than the Bank of Human Worth. Parents are released to accept and to encourage their children to discover the grand purpose for which God created them. A biblical lens leads us to emphasize *character building* over performance building. Then we will focus on raising champions for God, rather than fighting for the "survival of the fittest."

God's Currency

Psalm 127 has been called the Family, or Building, Psalm. David probably wrote it for his son, Solomon.

> Unless the LORD builds the house,
> They labor in vain who build it;
> Unless the LORD guards the city,
> The watchman keeps awake in vain.
> It is vain for you to rise up early,
> To retire late,
> To eat the bread of painful labors;
> For He gives to His beloved even in his sleep. (vv. 1–2 NASB)

Approaching parenthood without God is futility. On the other hand, our labor will be successful when we allow God to shape and guard the lives of our children. Unlike the Bank of Human Worth, God has a different currency for evaluating our children.

> Behold, children are a gift of the LORD;
> The fruit of the womb is a reward.
> Like arrows in the hand of a warrior,
> So are the children of one's youth.
> How blessed is the man whose quiver is full of them;
> They shall not be ashamed,
> When they speak with their enemies in the gate.
> (Ps. 127:3–5 NASB)

ADOPTING GOD'S VISION FOR CHILDREN

Have you considered lately the universe in which we live? Did you know that the sun is so large it could hold one million of our earths within it? That there are stars out in space that could hold 500 million suns the size of ours? That the galaxy to which our sun belongs contains 100 billion stars? That there are 100 billion other galaxies in the universe? If the thickness of this page represented the distance from the earth to the sun (93 million miles), the distance from the earth to the nearest star would be a stack of paper seventy-one feet high? Our universe is awesome, but the Bible says God is so awesome that even the highest heavens can't contain Him. "Behold, heaven and the heaven of heavens cannot contain You" (1 Kings 8:27 NKJV). It is humbling to consider that God says you are the ultimate within His creation!

Children Are Gifts

On the day that I (Elaine) turned five, my younger sister was born. I remember everyone saying, "Look at your little birthday present!" For some reason, I don't have any other early memories of Amy, except sharing "twin birthdays" and getting to pick out the birthday cake every other year. Evidently, my importance in the family seemed a bit threatened. Never underestimate the impact of a well-planned birthday party. Two years later, I remember standing outside our gate until I was led into a backyard carnival—complete with games and a magic show performed by my older cousins. I have no idea what presents I received, other than the "gift" of significance given to me by my parents that day. God says children are "gifts," to be accepted and treasured. Some Bible translations use the word *heritage,* from the same root as *heirloom.* An heirloom is a priceless item that cannot be appraised in monetary terms because the value is not only in the item itself, but also in its origin. David has a beautiful hand-stitched quilt that is different from the ones his grandmother made for each grandchild. I have a ring my grandmother gave me, containing diamonds worn by three generations of women in her family. If we sold these items, we could never recover their true value because their origin makes them priceless. When we realize the tremendous potential God sees in our children, we will care for them as precious gifts whose value actually increases from generation to generation.

Children Are Rewards

When we are tired and off guard, children may seem more like dubious blessings than valuable rewards. The number of abandoned and aborted babies reveals our society's belief that children are penalties for poor family planning. Children with disabilities are often labeled "mistakes" rather than prizes. When Amanda was eight, she brought home a trophy from basketball camp and announced, "This is my first reward!" Even though she was the tallest girl her age, we knew she wasn't chosen "Best Camper" because she was the top shooter or ball handler in the bunch. Amanda was born with a rare genetic syndrome affecting her growth and motor development. Her first five years were filled with painful tests, surgeries, and physical therapy. Despite our resolve to provide every possible intervention, we struggled to understand the "reward" of a suffering child. When Amanda was five, we visited Disneyworld and Cinderella's castle. Cinderella was swamped with children wanting her autograph, but Amanda finally had her turn for a brief conversation and a picture. Later that afternoon, she rested on the curb while the other tourists watched the parade of Disney characters passing by. Eventually, Cinderella's sparkling carriage arrived, with the smiling actress waving gracefully. Amid the sea of people, one particular child caught her eye. She leaned out of the window and called, "Hello, Amanda!" The character our daughter most admired for her outward beauty and grace had recognized her for very different reasons—a contagious smile, a determined spirit, and the gift of compassion. Years later, the basketball trophy stands alone on her desk hutch—our constant reminder that *every* child is a reward—and even imperfect bodies cannot diminish the qualities God will reveal to those who have eyes to see them.

Children Are Arrows

In the movie *Forest Gump*, the opening scene follows a feather floating along in the wind. It appears to be a symbol of destiny or fate throughout the film. Viewers are subtly given the idea that our lives are like feathers driven along by the winds of circumstance. On the contrary, Psalm 139 states that God has an intentional design for our lives before we are born. "Your eyes saw my substance, being yet unformed. And in Your book they all were written, The days fashioned for me, When as yet there were none of them" (Ps. 139:16 NKJV). God says children are arrows, not feathers. Since most of you are not bow hunters, there are several concepts about arrows needing explanation. "Like arrows in the hand of a warrior" infers the threat of a battle (Ps. 127:4 NKJV). A look at the news substantiates that a war is raging on many levels. A parent's first reaction is to shield a child—and certainly we must protect them as long as possible. But this illustration implies that parents must eventually send children into the battle.

An arrow must be straight. Bows and arrows were the principal offensive weapon during biblical times. The arrow was made of very light wood and winged with three rows of feathers to make it spin and fly steady and straight. Without a straight arrow, the warrior had no chance of hitting his target. You may have heard the phrase "straight as an arrow," in reference to someone with high morals. The first step for parents is to shape the character of the child while the will is most pliable.

An arrow must be aimed. The Hebrew archer was highly trained because of the difficulty of shooting the powerful bows made from wood and animal horns. The archer never fired his arrows randomly or haphazardly, but made every arrow count. We are responsible for more than hit-or-miss parenting. We must aim and guide our children toward the right target. All children are unique, and though we cannot imagine God's full plan for them, we should carefully aim them in His direction.

An arrow must be released. If the arrow is never released, it cannot accomplish its purpose. We do not own our children. God has entrusted them to us for a few fleeting years. The day you release your children into the world may seem a long way off, but you must release them spiritually, emotionally, and physically one day at a time. To the baby-sitter. To school. To camp. To college. To the world. Children have so many more opportunities today. Some are risks. Parents must discern the difference without letting their fears hold them back. The arrow, when aimed properly and released, can hit a target that the warrior cannot reach. A wise man once said, "Children are the living messages we send to a time we will not see." What a tremendous blessing to know that our children have the potential to achieve things we will never be able to accomplish!

SHAPING THE NEXT GENERATION

Throughout the Bible, God uses other rich word pictures to express important life principles. One is the analogy of a potter and clay representing God and His children. "But now, O LORD, You are our Father; we are the clay, and You our potter; and all we are the work of Your hand" (Isa. 64:8 NKJV). From the beginning, the potter has in mind what he wants to make. The clay must be prepared and purified before it is put on the potter's wheel. It must be worked to become pliable and its molecules "awakened" so it won't stiffen up and become breakable. Shaping the clay requires the turning and tension of the spinning wheel, but it is the potter's hands that transform the lump into vessels for different functions. If the potter removes his hands and walks away, the wheel continues spinning and the clay loses its shape.

God is both Father and Potter, already at work shaping your children (and their parents). His gracious plan includes you in the awesome process. Sooner than most, Moses' parents had to release their son, but it is striking how permanently they influenced him during their brief window of opportunity. Though he was adopted by Pharaoh's daughter and raised in luxury by learned teachers, it was his earliest influences that held strong. Is it really possible to shape a generation? To significantly influence its values and direction? Some speculate that culture exerts the primary influence on a generation. Although teachers, coaches, grandparents, and friends will significantly influence your children's lives, God intends for parents to fulfill this role. By faith, like Moses' parents, you can raise your children in any cultural or political climate. Parents have the overwhelming but fulfilling challenge of "awakening" and preparing their children—and placing them in God's hands to be fashioned as He desires. We don't know who our children are meant to be in their generation, but parents with God's vision can raise children with vision. He already knows their unique purpose within their generation. It is your calling—and ours—to help this generation of children discover the unique and wondrous plans their heavenly Father has for their lives. Plans for hope. Plans for His glory. "This will be written for the generation to come, That a people yet to be created may praise the LORD" (Ps. 102:18 NKJV).

A parent's prayer . . . Lord, you know my heart better than anyone (including myself). You know how stressed out I get at times, just thinking about all of the dangers and unknowns my children will face. I hate being a worrier, and yet there truly is a great deal to be concerned about. I fear for their safety, but I also fear for their souls. This world is so seductive and appealing. I often wonder if there will be others in their generation who will stand for Christ. Lord, change my attitude. Give me the kind of hope that only You can give. I want to see my children from Your vantage point. I do see them as gifts and rewards, but not the way You do. There are moments when I catch a glimpse of Your potential in them. Magnify those pictures in my heart and mind. Burn Your vision for them in my heart. I must confess, I am having trouble picturing them as arrows. It's hard to imagine making their lunches, giving them a hug and then sending them out into "battle." Yet, I know this is Your way. Let Your Word do its work in me, now, because I know time is short.

DISCUSSION QUESTIONS

1. What are your greatest fears as a parent?

2. What factors tend to create anxiety in your parenting? What factors tend to lead you toward peace in your parenting?

3. Would you describe the family in which you grew up as primarily "cultural" (world's lens) or "biblical" (God's lens)? Explain your response. How do you view your family today?

4. Name some ways you have "bought into" the cultural view of children.

5. Describe what a biblical family should look like in today's culture.

2 } What Did You Expect?

> *"Now to Him who is able to do exceedingly abundantly above all that we ask or think, according to the power that works in us, to Him be glory in the church by Christ Jesus to all generations, forever and ever. Amen."*
> —*Ephesians 3:20–21 NKJV*

As children, many of us dreamed what parenthood would be like, but never as much as during pregnancy or when anticipating adoption. No wonder people say, "We're expecting!" We imagined strolling the baby in the park, quiet evenings rocking by the fireplace, building sand castles on the beach, and squeals of laughter during tickle matches. Everyone has a vision of what parenthood will be like . . . more or less. How much our dreams would differ from reality never entered our minds! We were shocked to realize the complex demands children bring when they burst into our world. That brings to mind a woman who telephoned a friend and asked how she was feeling. "Terrible" came the reply. "My head's splitting, and my back and legs are killing me . . . and the house is a mess, and the kids are simply driving me crazy." Very sympathetically, the caller said, "Listen, go and lie down. I'll come over right away and cook lunch for you, clean up the house, and take care of the children while you get some rest. By the way, how is Sam?"

"Sam?" the complaining housewife gasped. "Who is Sam?"

"My heavens," exclaimed the first woman, "I must have dialed the wrong number!"

There was a long pause. "Are you still coming over?" the harried mother asked hopefully.[1]

CHILDREN BRING CHANGES . . . MORE OR LESS

It is a fact of life that children mean *more*—and children mean *less*. They mean more expenses, more noise, and more messes—but also more love, more laughter, and more fun! Children mean less sleep, less energy, and less leisure time—but also less loneliness, less idleness, and less boredom! We divide our married life into two parts—B.C. (before children) and A.D. (after delivery). In B.C., we might be sitting at home at 9:00 P.M. and decide at the last minute to go to a late movie. We would call friends to meet us for pizza and stay out until after midnight. We loved the spontaneity and freedom! However, many of our friends already had children so we thought we wanted to join the "club." We began praying that God would bring children into our home. One month later Elaine was pregnant—I (David) had hoped for more time to work on it! She couldn't wait to wear maternity clothes so everyone would know we were expecting. Little did she know how people would notice! By her third month, strangers asked if she was near delivery. Before long the doctor confirmed their suspicions—twins! Our expectations changed again. Neither of us had ever changed a diaper. We had only held a newborn once. After the initial shock, Elaine attended a multiples meeting to get advice. We read books about childbirth, baby care, and discipline. Friends and family helped us acquire double of everything we thought we might need. We picked four names for Baby A (girl or boy) and Baby B (girl or boy). For all our preparation, things *still* didn't turn out as we expected! Two months before the due date, Elaine was hospitalized for toxemia and early labor. Three weeks later, Blake and

Joel made their entrance into the world, requiring fifteen critical days in intensive care. When we began living in A.D., things changed dramatically. Sometimes it took Elaine days to find two baby-sitters so we could "get out." By the time I picked up the baby-sitters and Elaine completed her forty-five-minute seminar on baby care, we often lost our appetite and were too tired to go anywhere. We were beginning to realize that the journey of parenthood is rarely what we anticipate!

READY OR NOT . . . ADJUST!

Has parenthood been harder than you thought it would be? No one has to tell parents of preschoolers that children force us to make daily adjustments! Why do we resist the sacrifices parenthood requires? Perhaps it is our natural tendency to be self-directed and our innate desire to be in control. Children have a way of making us feel completely out of control! Parenthood is often the first time we have to be selfless, because young children require so much energy and focus. Babies are totally self-centered until around the age of four or five when they discover that the universe does not revolve around them. It is normal to have days where fatigue and frustration cause you to feel discontented and even wonder why you ever had children. We must be careful not to let this attitude go unchecked. Even in circumstances outside your control, there are always choices within your control. As you meet the challenges of parenting, you can choose to adjust to your circumstances in one of two ways: willingly or unwillingly—but you will adjust. Paul was a person who knew firsthand about learning how to get along with more—or less. He made a statement that surely relates to "adjusting" parents: "I have learned to be content in whatever circumstances I am . . . in any and every circumstance I have learned the secret of being filled and going hungry, both of having abundance and suffering need. I can do all things through Him who strengthens me" (Phil. 4:11–13 NASB).

Obviously, it was Paul's dramatic encounter with Jesus that changed his outlook on the continual ups and downs of life.

SEEKING SELFLESSNESS

Five-year-old Matthew saw that there was only a little chocolate milk left in the carton, so he announced: "Mom, I'm going to have to drink this all by myself because there's not enough for Christine, too." Dad overheard this and said sternly, "Matthew, if Jesus were here, what would He do?" Without hesitation, little Christine answered for him. "If Jesus were here, He'd make more chocolate milk!"[2] There will be days when you feel as if there isn't enough of you to go around, and you have nothing left to give your spouse or children. Even Christian parents fall into believing that parenting is merely a lesson in survival. God has far greater confidence in you! True contentment is not found in selfishness but in *selfless*ness. Jesus provided the ultimate example. He laid aside the privileges that belonged to Him for our sakes. He should have been treated as a king, but His life was one of humility and humiliation. Philippians 2:1–10 says He did not demand to dominate, but quietly served others—ultimately giving His very life for us on the cross. We are reminded to "let this mind be in you which was also in Christ Jesus" (Phil. 2:5 NKJV).

Parents tend to look forward to the day when the children won't need them quite so much. It's funny that in God's economy of opposites, He actually looks forward to the day when His children surrender and cry, "I can't do one more thing without You!" He probably just smiles and thinks, *You finally get it! Apart from Me you can do nothing—and with Me, nothing is impossible!* Your submission to "selflessness" does not mean you abandon your individual personhood—but there will be several seasons of parenthood when your children will need more of you than others. You will begin to see how much your child's disposition and outlook on life are influenced by the attitudes you adopt, the expectations you take up, and the choices you make. When you begin to *willingly* empty yourself out for your children, and *humbly* go to God for refilling, He will empower you to *joyfully* invest yourself into your family.

IDENTIFYING YOUR EXPECTATIONS

"Listen to that strong voice. I'll bet he'll be a preacher like his grandfather!" "Look at those long, delicate fingers. Maybe she'll be a pianist like Aunt Rose." "I heard she's so smart that she's already smiling. Maybe she'll be a doctor like her daddy." So goes the conversation on every maternity ward on the planet! *Expect* means "to anticipate or hope for a certain response, result, or behavior." We all have hopes and dreams for our children. Some common fantasies include exceptional beauty, unusual intelligence, great importance, athletic or material success, popularity, high achievement—and, of course, good health. Today's couples have many more options allowing control over the circumstances surrounding childbearing and adoption. Some carefully calculate when conception will occur—books claim you can determine the sex of your child. Parents can choose any type of delivery from general anesthesia to general audiences! Genetic engineering is no longer science fiction. Doctors can even perform surgery in the womb—yet so many choices make it easy to ignore the One who ultimately determines the due date, sex, and exact combinations of genes and chromosomes. God ordered your daughter's nose, your son's dimples, and the family characteristics connecting them to previous generations. He "pre-wired" their temperament and capabilities before you ever discovered them.

> You are the one who put me together inside my mother's body,
> and I praise you because of the wonderful way you created me.
> Everything you do is marvelous!
> Of this I have no doubt. (Ps. 139:13–14 CEV)

EXPLORING YOUR EXPECTATIONS

As you pinpoint your dreams and expectations for your children it is important to investigate their sources. Most can be traced back to family background, past experiences, or cultural influences. You may have fond memories of childhood experiences that you seek to duplicate for your own children—or you may desperately want to avoid the experiences you had. I (Elaine) actually made a little book entitled, "What I Will Not Do as A Parent"— most of which I've done over the years. David somehow formed the opinion that an odd number of children was better—fifteen years later, he still thinks *five* is a good odd number! As children spend more time away from home, they observe other family dynamics and begin to evaluate their own family structure for the first time. A young person from an unhealthy background may become quite disturbed when the environment that he thought was "typical" is shown to be anything but the ideal family. Once recognized, the patterns established by our own parents can be far more difficult to change than you would think. Chapter Four will further discuss the impact of past experiences on parenting style, and how our early years become a primary source of our expectations for the next generation.

Cultural trends also influence your hopes and plans even more than you may recognize. There is an unspoken desire for our child to walk first, look the best, and win the most. You probably have friends who dress their children like mini-adults, or enroll them in a different structured activity every day—and that's at the ripe old age of five! You may feel the pressure to follow their lead, since parents fear that their child will be left behind if they don't get a head start on everything their peers are doing. Parents should provide as many rich experiences as possible without succumbing to the urgency to produce highly specialized, narrowly focused children who can become overburdened and unbalanced.

EXAMINING YOUR MOTIVES

In every sport or activity our children have participated in, there has always been at least one overzealous parent who makes what should be a childhood pastime a disagreeable experience. Particularly in sports, you must usually endure a parent who screams at their child (or yours) as if that peewee soccer game were the World Cup. In one music studio, second-graders were already grouped by who seemed to have the promise to become musical pedagogues. It is natural for parents to anticipate the future and hope for the best. You should give your children wings to reach their highest God-given potential. But dreams can become demands if your motives are wrong. Maybe your own parents pushed you too much to excel. You may even catch yourself pressuring your children to "perform" for you. How would you answer these soul-searching questions today: *Am I emphasizing performance over character? Are my dreams for my child to fulfill unmet goals of my own? Are my goals the same as my child's? Am I helping or forcing my child to "reach for the stars"?*

Look deep into my heart, God,
   and find out everything I am thinking.
Don't let me follow evil ways,
   but lead me in the way that time has proven true.
(Ps. 139:23–24 CEV)

ACCEPTING THE UNEXPECTED

Have your children lived up to your expectations, or are you secretly disappointed with the child God has given you? Maybe you wanted a girl with curly red hair, but got a boy with no hair at all. You probably told yourself that it really didn't matter "as long as the baby is healthy." That brings up another burdensome question: What happens when dreams become nightmares? You are probably acquainted with parents who have faced unexpected, even tragic circumstances with their children. You may have experienced, in some degree, the anguish that illness, impairment, or even inadequacy brings. Illness may include anything from prematurity or delivery problems to chronic ear infections or a life-threatening disease. Children are not exempt from injuries or illnesses resulting in physical or mental impairments ranging from mild to profound. More commonly, some children are judged *inadequate* according to the world's standards. An unattractive appearance, awkward social behaviors, or the apparent lack of any talent or aptitude usually equals "loser" in our society. It seems no one is satisfied with an average, "garden-variety" child. If your expectations and motives have been out of balance for a long time, you may be feeling discontent, disappointment, even despair when you look at your struggling son or daughter. These are the very children who need the gracious acceptance and tender redirection of their parents. We must hold a "funeral" memorializing the "death" of the perfect child. That will free us to discover and celebrate the unique individuals God has called us to motivate toward excellence. Improper expectations may require more than a child can possibly give; while proper expectations will ignite more than a parent can possibly imagine!

Your Dreams or God's?

The scenario has become too familiar, and this time it hit too close to home. Last summer, an outstanding former high school athlete in our community took his own life on the morning his parents were to take him to college where he hoped to play football before getting his chance in the NFL. While they loaded the car, he went inside to get something he had forgotten, and instead, shot himself. Neither relatives, friends, nor former coaches could imagine how someone so talented, positive, and respected would choose death over life. What they didn't know, was that he had never even sent in the application or his transcripts for admission. After high school he didn't have the grades to play at a Division I school, and was forced to go to a junior college to become eligible to play. When he began struggling there, he quietly dropped out without ever telling his teachers or family.

Evidently, he played out the only script that he thought would please the people who had always told him: "You're going to be great. You're going to the NFL." He never understood that football—or any other sport or achievement—is not the only measure of a person's value in life, or reason for living.[3]

Correctly Defining Success

What is the proper standard for measuring success in our children—and what defines *success*, anyway? Words like *popularity, achievement,* and *prosperity* come to mind immediately. Good character, contentment, and fulfillment are not as readily named. The secret of true contentment with your children lies in keeping your eyes on God's priorities rather than on our culture's definition of success. That brings to mind another youth who was exceptionally strong and talented. His physical skills were unsurpassed by anyone around. As he grew older, he was the winner of all the athletic contests; in fact, he was known throughout his whole country and his friends and neighbors began calling him, "The Champion." In another place, there was a young boy who was just a regular kid, the youngest of eight brothers. No one seemed to notice him, except when they gave him the least desirable chores. However, this young man had a father who instilled godly character in him, and invested much time in instructing him about life. One day, the young boy was brought face-to-face with "The Champion" and something very unexpected happened. The real champion emerged. By now you may recognize the story of David and Goliath. By outside appearances, Goliath was the "winner," but in the end, the unknown boy named David was revealed as the true victor. The difference? Matters of the heart.

On another day, the prophet Samuel examined Jesse's seven oldest sons to determine who would be God's anointed king. Even Jesse never considered his youngest son a possibility for the throne. God reminded Samuel and Jesse of a crucial lesson that parents need to remember: "But the LORD said to Samuel, 'Do not look at his appearance or at his physical stature, because I have refused him [the older brothers]. For the LORD does not see as man sees; for man looks at the outward appearance, but the LORD looks at the heart,'" (1 Sam. 16:7 NKJV).

GREAT EXPECTATIONS

Time is running out for my friend. We are sitting at lunch when she casually mentions that she and her husband are thinking of "starting a family." What she means is that her biological clock has begun its countdown and she is being forced to consider the prospect of motherhood. "We're taking a survey," she says, half joking. "Do you think I should have a baby?"

"It will change your life," I say carefully, keeping my tone neutral.

"I know," she says. "No more sleeping in on Saturdays, no more spontaneous vacations . . ."

But that is not what I mean at all. I look at my friend, trying to decide what to tell her. I want her to know what she will never learn in childbirth classes. I want to tell her that the physical wounds of childbearing heal, but that becoming a mother will leave her with an emotional wound so raw that she will be forever vulnerable. I consider warning her that she will never read a newspaper again without asking, "What if that had been my child?" That every plane crash, every fire will haunt her. That when she sees pictures of starving children, she will look at the mothers and wonder if anything could be worse than watching your child die. I want my friend to know that everyday, routine decisions will no longer be routine. That a visit to McDonald's and a five-year-old boy's understandable desire to go to the men's room rather than the women's will become a major dilemma. That right there, in the midst of clattering trays and screaming children, issues of independence will be weighed against the prospect that a child molester may be lurking in the rest room.

Looking at my attractive friend, I want to assure her that eventually she will shed the pounds of pregnancy, but she will never feel the same way about herself. That she would give it up in a moment to save her offspring, but will also begin to hope for more years, not so much to accomplish her own dreams but to watch her child accomplish his. My friend's relationship with her husband will change, I know, but not in the way she thinks. I wish she could understand how much more you can love a man who is always careful to powder the baby or who never hesitates to play "bad guys" with his son. I think she should know that she will fall in love with her husband again for reasons she would now find very unromantic. My friend's quizzical look makes me realize that tears have formed in my eyes. "You'll never regret it," I say finally. Then I reach across the table and, squeezing my friend's hand, I offer a prayer for her and me and all the mere mortal women who stumble their way into this holiest of callings.

A parent's prayer . . . God, I am struck by the magnitude of unrealistic expectations I have brought into parenting, and burdened my children with. I realize that some expectations are good—like hoping to see certain character traits and spiritual qualities develop in their lives. I must be so careful not to play Your role in their lives. Teach me how to guide without dictating. Help me to be honest enough with You and myself to check my motives. There is no question that my life was forever changed the moment each of the children arrived. It has been an exciting experience as well as a wearisome one. I am beginning to see Your divine destiny for me emerge—and the reward of giving myself to them each day. Lord, You know that I am clueless about what to expect tomorrow, so I will trust You to prepare me for the next surprise in my parenting journey.

DISCUSSION QUESTIONS

1. How would you describe the "more and less" parenting has brought to your life?

2. What has been the greatest adjustment you have had to make as a parent?

3. Unmistakably, our dreams are not always God's plans. How have your dreams differed from reality?

4. How do you think your current attitude is impacting your child's disposition?

5. How have you overemphasized the performance of your children compared to emphasizing their character?

3 } Mastering the Hat Trick

> *"For the eyes of the LORD move to and fro throughout the earth that He may strongly support those whose heart is completely His."*
> —*2 Chronicles 16:9 NASB*

Try this riddle. What do a sun visor, ball cap, chef's hood, fireman's helmet, swami's turban, and chauffeur's cap have in common? *Answer:* They are just a few of the hats parents must put on every day! One of the most challenging tasks of adulthood is mastering the hat trick—balancing our changing roles as individual, spouse, and parent. The hat trick is a constant juggling act. We can botch it and risk destroying our marriages, our families, and our own lives—but as we become proficient at it, we will continue growing into a complete person while enriching the lives of others.

THE "HATS" OF PARENTING

David's "Hard Hat"

I grew up in a pastor's home between two sisters. During my eighteen years there, I practiced my roles as son, brother, student, friend, and Christian disciple. During college, I prepared for a career in business. Next I went to work for a homebuilder. I remember my excitement when I picked out my own apartment and bought a new car. A year later I bought my first home. I made my own decisions about how I spent my time and with whom I would spend it. Life was great!

Elaine's "Diamond Tiara"

I was the stereotypical middle child between two sisters. During my years at home, I grew in my roles as daughter, sister, student, friend, and young Christian. In college, I prepared for a career in communication disorders. After graduate school, I moved eight hundred miles away to complete a clinical fellowship. For the first time, I owned a car, lived alone, and had no one telling me what to do. The freedom was both exhilarating and frightening!

Top Hat and Wedding Veil

We met our junior year in college and dated until after we graduated. Our parents had instilled the conviction that marriage is forever—and David was willing to wait almost that long to find the "perfect" person. Three and a half years later, we finally got married. Our relationship was built on mutual faith, friendship, and common goals, so marriage was fulfilling for both of us. We continued our separate careers, our individual interests, and our different responsibilities—but now we worked together on community projects and ministries within our church. We maintained old friendships, but developed new ones with people we both enjoyed. At the same time, we were learning new lessons about relating to others as colleagues, bosses, in-laws, and grown children. Balancing all of those roles took a lot of hard work!

We spent about three years practicing our roles as spouses before we added the most complex role of all!

Fire Helmet and Nurse's Cap

Three children within twenty-two months certainly brought a lot of excitement and exhaustion into our home! Suddenly we multiplied the number of "individuals" living under one roof. We were cast as "Mommy" and "Daddy" with little dress rehearsal. Unfortunately, we can't "pause-play" our roles as individuals and spouses while we practice our mothering and fathering roles. The alarm still went off every morning, signaling another workday. I (Elaine) chose to work at home—and juggling three in diapers was much more stressful than a caseload of patients. David was building a new business and was absorbed in supporting a growing family. When he came home in the evening, a variety of "hats" awaited him. He wanted to escape to the television, but I developed what he called a "wild" look in my eyes. I needed adult conversation. He needed individual attention. The children needed parental affection. David's friends needed a golf partner. My friends needed a walking buddy. The church needed youth leaders. The demands seemed impossible.

FELLOW HAT JUGGLERS

Throughout Scripture, there are many heroic men and women, but few of them mastered their roles in all three areas. Abraham, "father of many nations," struggled to master the hat trick. It took him a lifetime to learn to walk by faith. He loved Sarah, yet repeatedly jeopardized her life because of his own fears. They struggled through years of infertility and taking matters into their own hands. However, all accounts indicate that Abraham became an excellent father. Rebekah had problems mastering the hat trick. She was an obedient young woman of faith when she married Isaac. Her sons were born after much prayer, but she played favorites with Jacob. Ultimately, she caused him to deceive his brother and father. Later, Jacob demonstrated integrity problems, and got some of his own medicine when he ended up with the wrong wife! He became a father of vision, but had difficulty handling the conflicts between his twelve sons. David was one of the greatest men chronicled in Scripture, yet he never fully integrated his roles personally, as husband or father. What a relief for those of us who struggle to maintain balance in our lives.

Honorable Mention

Job was one who seems to have mastered the hat trick in all three areas. *Suffering* is the word generally associated with Job's name, but his life provides a model of so much more. *Job mastered his role as an individual*—he was "blameless in his time." His faith was influential and consistent. *Job mastered his role as a father*—family was his top priority. We are told about his family before his wealth, success, or prestige. Job had ten grown children who still loved one another. He never stopped praying for them, even as adults. *Job mastered his role as a spouse*—his marriage weathered the worst of circumstances. Mrs. Job's emotional struggle after losing all ten children, their wealth, and Job's health, teaches us about honesty during difficult seasons of life. In the end, God restored Job's health, their possessions, their intimacy, and their family. What an example to strive for! As we settle into marriage and family life, it is helpful to have other couples for encouragement, support, and advice.

BALANCING YOUR INDIVIDUALITY

When was the last time you said, "I love my life"? Especially during the early parenting years, your role as an individual is easily neglected. Boundaries can become blurred. Moms feel pulled by the constant needs of children, plus household—and often workplace—demands. Most working moms still do most of the daily household and parenting tasks along with their outside jobs. Contrary to popular belief, women who stay home with children are "working women," too! Men are often at a critical point in their careers when children arrive. The corporate trend of downsizing has doubled everyone's workload and raised concern about job security. They may be thinking, *Doesn't anybody appreciate how hard I work?* Meanwhile, women are wondering, *What about my needs?* Unfortunately, there's little time to ponder those questions in a busy home!

One of the first issues of parenthood is daily care of the baby. More couples are downsizing their life-style since the first few years are so important for physical, intellectual, emotional, and spiritual development of a child. Putting a career, a promotion, a transfer, or a bigger house on hold is one of the most difficult sacrifices parents will make. Home offices, shared jobs, and flextime allow more options for pursuing a vocation once children go to school. In just a few years, there will be no more car pools, field trips, or ball games to interrupt our careers and pastimes—and we can resume our goals outside our empty nests. Until then, you must not only *maintain* your identity, but continue *growing up* as a person. This is a continuing lesson in time management and the art of compromise! Remain vigilant about your spiritual, emotional, and physical health—in that order. Aim to keep learning, participate in worthy projects, exercise where they offer childcare, and take regular "time-outs" for adult conversation. As you protect time for your private world, devise a workable life-style of personal discipline, and accept your limits during changing seasons of life, you will flourish in your other roles as well.

BALANCING YOUR PARTNERSHIP

Children certainly bring joy to a marriage, but they also introduce new physical, financial, and emotional pressures to the relationship. As precious as they are, babies can drive a wedge between a husband and wife. Husbands say their wives are oblivious to their needs for attention and affection. Wives say they have little time or energy for intimacy, much less for themselves. Physical intimacy begins with meaningful conversation, which is more difficult when parents are tired or preoccupied. Unfortunately, many men believe they have "earned" the right to relax or to be released from parental responsibility after work hours. No wonder our relationships are so easily weakened! Both spouses must learn and apply the secret of marriage building: "Be sincere in your love for others. Hate everything that is evil and hold tight to everything that is good. Love each other as brothers and sisters and honor others more than you do yourself" (Rom. 12:9–10 CEV). It is vital to establish—from the first day home—that nurturing your marriage will not be thrown away with the diapers.

However, a pattern as old as sin has reached an all-time peak—an epidemic of push-pull marriages where neither partner fulfills their God-given role.

Husbands

God compares your leadership to Christ's: "A husband is the head of his wife as Christ is the head and the Savior of the church . . . A husband should love his wife as much as Christ loved the church and gave his life for it . . . A husband should love his wife as much as he loves himself" (Eph. 5:23, 25, 28 CEV). So many of us focus on the *head* aspect that we forget that Jesus did not dominate others, or force His ideas on them. He was a compassionate, accepting, and affectionate leader—never pushing His way into the limelight or demanding that His needs be met first. Just before defining a wife's role, Peter called Jesus the "Shepherd and Guardian of your souls" (1 Peter 2:25 NASB). The Eastern shepherd did not resemble our concept of cowboys. They did not drive their sheep from behind, mounted above them on horses. Instead, they walked along with them, directing them with a few quiet words. They fed, sheltered, defended, and provided rest for the sheep in their care. What woman would not respond to that kind of *servant* leadership?

A servant leader will take action and team up to complete more parenting and household tasks. Ordering your day to get home for dinner is a boundary only you can draw. Calling home to ask if she needs anything says you're thinking of her needs. Playing outside with the kids, or making tomorrow's round of bottles (without being asked), says you value your wife's time. She will be much more cordial and responsive when you automatically pitch in at dinnertime, bath time, and bedtime. Volunteer to keep the children *regularly* so she can run errands, attend meetings, and spend time with friends. She will be much more understanding when your agenda doesn't always come out on top! When she has time to go for a jog, take a bath, or read a magazine, you will find her offering the breaks you need! Tell her *constantly* how much you appreciate what she does for your family—especially the "little" things. Dates are a must—weekly, if possible. If you really want her attention, line up the baby-sitter and plan the date yourself! We know some couples who take turns spending the night at each other's houses. One family brings their children for a camp-in at your house, while you and your spouse get *their* house to yourselves. Great concept—especially when it's your turn away!

Wives

God compares your "followship" to sheep following a shepherd's lead. The analogy does not paint a picture of a suppressed or neglected wife—when the husband has truly mastered his role. However, Peter warned of our tendency to demand independence: "For you were continually straying like sheep, but now you have returned to the Shepherd and Guardian of your souls. In the same way, you wives, be submissive to your own husbands so that even if any of them are disobedient to the word, they may be won without a word by the behavior of their wives, as they observe your chaste and respectful behavior" (1 Peter 2:25–3:2 NASB). The Bible never depicts women as weak or inadequate. In Proverbs, a good wife is called a rare and valuable gem—competent, diligent, organized, shrewd, creative, and generous. She doesn't sit on the sidelines. She isn't a slave or restrained from communicating her opinions and desires. Because her husband has full confidence in her, a *responsive* wife continually devises ways to honor and enrich her husband (see Prov. 31:12).

You may have to organize and reprioritize to reserve time and energy for your husband. Even though you are tired, don't forget that he also deserves time to "veg out." Simply getting the children to bed early can save your romance! Instead of being so task-oriented, give each other permission to leave the dishes or post-pone the bills to spend at least one uninterrupted hour together each evening. If something just can't wait, work on necessary tasks together. Just having each other's company will strengthen your relationship as a partnership. One more tip: Husbands (like wives) need large doses of praise and affirmation. Try to focus on every-thing he *does* do right each day!

Couples

Children won't wait, but neither will marriages. Marital stress during parenthood is typical, but it doesn't have to be the rule if you learn to master your role as a marriage partner. Don't ratio-nalize that things will get better when the kids go to school, or during the teenage years, or when they finally leave the nest. Honor each other while there is still time. Remember what first attracted you to your mate. Ministry—not manipulation—is the key. If your marriage is on shaky ground, do not be afraid to seek support and counsel. If your spouse will not get help, at least you will learn new ways to respond. If you are considering bailing out, please talk to some divorced moms, dads, and children first. Most will tell you that the effects on your family are usually harder than the work it takes to restore a relationship. Finally, don't forget that the same God who made His Son come alive again can bring a dead marriage back to life—and even renew the passion of your youth!

JUGGLING YOUR ROLE AS A DAD

One day Elaine called my younger sister, Dawn, and her husband, Rick, answered the phone. She heard noise in the background and asked if he was baby-sitting their two-year-old triplets (see, things could be worse!). Rick's blunt response should be recorded in the Father's Hall of Fame: "No, I'm *fathering*." What a concept! Why is it that moms are mothering, and dads are "baby-sitting"? The world needs more dads like my brother-in-law, with the attitude that fatherhood is the most noble role in which you will ever engage.

Dads Mirror the Heavenly Father

One way God chose to reveal Himself was as a Father. The first institution He established was the family. Fathers provide the first glimpse of what God is like for their children. Many people have difficulty relating to a loving, interested heavenly Father, because they never saw it demonstrated at home. Children need dads who are personally involved in their lives. They need to know you will keep your promises. They shouldn't have to question your character or your good intentions for their welfare. What are you reflecting today?

Dads Set the Character Standard

Recently we were keeping the triplets. Anytime they observed something new, they would relate it to their dad. "My dad drinks coffee, too." "My dad has a hat, too." When he told them about planning their third birthday party at a place called "My Gym," they insisted from then on that they were going to "My Daddy's Gym!" Fathers have an awesome influence in their own homes. There is a brief window in the lives of young children for their father to become their greatest hero. Unfortunately, the importance of character has diminished in every arena of life. If dads fail to assume their biblical role, their kids will find another "star" to imitate.

Dads Minister and Instruct

Scripture clearly supports the father's role of providing for the family's needs. "But if anyone does not provide for his own, and especially for those of his household, he has denied the faith and is worse than an unbeliever" (1 Tim. 5:8 NKJV). However, providing for your family goes beyond material needs. Before they were made overseers of a congregation, elders had to demonstrate that they could manage their children well. Robert Wolgemuth, the author of *She Calls Me Daddy*, once said that no amount of success in business will ever make up for failure at home.[1] Dads are also charged with equipping their sons and daughters to live in today's world. They must sense when their children are discouraged, temper them when they become angry, direct them when they become confused, and reassure them when they become frightened. As evangelist Jay Strack once asked, "Are you man enough to be God's man?" Fathers need to ask themselves the same question every day.

> "So he shepherded them according to the integrity of his heart,
> And guided them by the skillfulness of his hands." (Ps. 78:72 NKJV)

What a responsibility—but the return will far outweigh the investment!

JUGGLING YOUR ROLE AS A MOM

Remember the phrase, "a face only a mother could love"? Even with limited experience, most women have the natural tendency to be protective, sympathetic, and nurturing toward children. The Bible has a lot to say about a mother's incomparable role. It is full of word pictures that compare other relationships to the tenderness, comfort, and love of a mother—but even in biblical times, it took the older women to encourage the younger women "to love their husbands, to love their children, to be discreet, chaste, homemakers, good, obedient to their own husbands, that the word of God may not be blasphemed" (Titus 2:4–5 NKJV). Think of the encouragement today's moms could use in the same area!

Mothers Are Nurturers

Most adults will agree that mothers are the glue that holds the home together. They are doctors, engineers, and attorneys all rolled into one tired body! A friend with three little ones put it this way: "I'm home full-time trying to be the elusive 'Super Mom.' I haven't attained that distinction yet, but I am on any given day Wendy, Lois Lane or Maid Marion . . . it's sometimes great, it's sometimes horrible, but nothing can compare with it."[2] In general, how do you introduce yourself? Too many times, women who do not work outside the home identify themselves as "just a mother." This reflects an identity crisis created by our culture, which has devalued the incredible influence a mother can have on her children. Children depend on their mothers for all their physical and emotional needs. Mothers are their child's advocate, best friend, counselor, and security guard—often all in the same day!

Mothers Are Team Teachers

According to Scripture, fathers prepare their sons for life in the world, but mothers are also in charge of training. "Listen, my son, to your father's instruction and do not forsake your mother's teaching" (Prov. 1:8 NIV). Ideally, both parents should instruct the children in matters of public and private life. Early childhood experts report that the greatest opportunity to influence character is before a child goes to school. This places a huge burden on the primary caregiver during the first five years. One working mom told me that her week at home when her child had chicken pox was the most *boring* week of her adult life. After cleaning out every closet and playing every game in the house, she couldn't see how anyone could stay at home full-time. Somewhere she missed that motherhood is more than cleaning and entertaining a young child. A mom on a mission can be as intellectually stimulated as the busiest executive! She knows that even filling a plastic pool for a backyard play group is a significant task for a "professor of life." Raising children is so much more than changing diapers, driving the car pool, or giving birthday parties. If we had the vision to see mothers as "generational engineers," we might gaze beyond the grape jelly and grass stains and recognize the awesome accomplishments so many mothers have inspired.

Mothers Are Dedicators

Hannah remains a perfect example of a mother who literally dedicated her only son to God. He only had three to eight years with her before being thrust into a compromising home environment. The book of 1 Samuel shows that prayer was already a significant part of her life before she became a mother. David has strong memories of his mom praying with him about God's calling on his life (and even the girl he would marry someday!). Praying mothers must be careful what they ask God to give or remove from their child's life—especially moms who have an agenda to help their child get ahead in the world. James and John's mother was like that. She came to Jesus and asked Him for a little favor: "Command that in Your kingdom these two sons of mine may sit, one on Your right and one on Your left." His answer probably shocked her. "You do not know what you are asking for" (Matt. 20:20–28 NASB). My friend Maureen has two grown sons, but she continues to take a mother's prayer seriously. She reminded me that our days to nurture and train our children will be over in the blink of an eye, but our role of dedicating them to God will never end, even throughout adulthood.

No Turning Back

We have to admit that there have been a few days when we would like to be relieved of our roles as mom and dad. I (Elaine) have told my children that I was going to box them up, wrap them up, and mail them away to Gammy's house. One time I even told David that I'd consider leaving him—except I'd probably be left alone with the kids!

I (David) have occasional thoughts of how nice it would be to escape from my responsibilities, or at least go play golf instead of coming home as I promised! Right now, your role as a mother or father may require the largest amount of your time and energy. This may be a season when the idea that you are an individual is a mist. There may be periods when your spouse seems more like your roommate than your lover. Three of the greatest gifts you can give each other are commitment, commitment, and *commitment*. In 1519, Hernando Cortez, along with seven hundred men, landed on the coast of Vera Cruz. His mission was to conquer Mexico and capture its vast treasures. After unloading the ships, Cortez instructed his men to burn all eleven ships. You see, he was on a mission and was serious about his commitment. The message was simple—"There is no turning back. We either succeed or we die."[3] Are you that committed to your spouse and your children today? The next several years will require a lot of flexibility, stamina, and hat changes—but you can learn to balance your ever-evolving roles with persistence and God's help. Until then, dig out your party hat, and determine to enjoy the journey!

A parent's prayer . . . Father, Your Word says that You know my thoughts before I even think them. I guess this means You are fully aware of how I have been feeling about life lately. I have so much to be thankful for and yet I am so tired. The word, "fatigue" doesn't do justice to the physical and emotional wear-and-tear I am experiencing right now. I know You said that there is a season for all things. But trying to wear all my hats at the same time seems impossible. I know I am out of balance. It's not that our marriage is bad, but I have let it grow stagnant. The trouble seems to be finding time to even talk. You know how needy the children are right now. My work has suffered because of my pace, and my health has paid a price. I am venting, Lord! I am calling out for help. You are the only One who can sustain me during these days. I don't know how long this season will last, but I ask You to keep pumping Your hope and Your strength into my veins. Help me to enjoy the moment, even now.

DISCUSSION QUESTIONS

1. Which of your primary roles (individual, spouse, parent) has been most dominant during the last year? Explain your response.

2. Which of your primary roles (individual, spouse, parent) has been the most difficult for you to master or balance during the last year? Explain your response.

3. How has parenting affected your marriage? Is it currently helping or hurting your relationship with your spouse?

4. In what ways have your role and your responsibilities as a parent affected your personal development as an individual? Try to identify both positives and negatives.

4 }

Stuck Between Past and Future

"Then I will make up to you for the years
That the swarming locust has eaten . . ."
—*Joel 2:25* NASB

Years ago, on a family ski trip, we were changing planes at the Chicago airport. The gate from which we were departing was on the opposite end of the airport from our arrival gate. Before we left, I had warned the children that they were responsible for carrying their own backpacks. After walking several yards, they began complaining, then moaning about how heavy their bags were. Before I knew it, I was covered with a variety of carry-on baggage, heavy jackets, and preschool "necessities." I thought I would collapse before reaching that gate! There is a different kind of baggage that is just as heavy—perhaps heavier. Though usually invisible to others, it makes every day an exhausting journey. We are referring to the effect of unresolved past issues that chain themselves to our souls. They come in a wide variety of sizes and shapes. You may be carrying some of them.

WHAT BAGS ARE IN YOUR CLOSET?

The Bag of "What-Ifs"
Ever ask yourself, *What if I had finished school? What if I had*

taken that other job? What if I had married someone else? What if I hadn't taken out that loan? Questions like these only weigh us down—we will never know the answers about what might have been.

The Bag of Disappointment

Everyone feels disheartened or disillusioned when someone close lets us down or circumstances don't change over time. Disappointment with ourselves is another common bag to add to the weight we already bear.

The Bag of Fear

Do you find yourself avoiding new opportunities because you cannot risk another fiasco? Fear of failure or loss of control causes people to escape or dominate uncomfortable situations. Chronic anxiety can lead to full-blown phobias that can affect your ability to care for yourself and others.

The Bag of Guilt

One of the heaviest bags a person can drag around is the bag of guilt. Inside may be *true guilt* over unconfessed sin before God or others, but *false guilt* that has been unjustly shouldered can have the same effect if not released.

The Bag of Criticism

Perhaps your parents, teachers, and peers were critical of you. No matter how hard you tried, it was never quite good enough. Your perfectionist tendencies may have their root in never feeling that you could measure up.

The Bag of Abuse

Physical, sexual—even ritual abuse plagues thousands of helpless children each year. Even verbal assaults like "You'll never amount to anything!" or "You make me sick!" can damage the spirit as deeply as bodily scars. Unless you have experienced the poison transmitted by abuse, it is difficult to comprehend its far-reaching effects. Sadly, if these wounds are not treated properly, an inclination may be developed to pass them on to others.

The Bag of Rejection

You may have been abandoned, neglected, or ignored during childhood. Now that you are an adult, you may continue to have feelings of insecurity, or need more assurance than others. If you were cast aside somewhere in your past, the chains may feel impossible to break.

ACCUMULATING NEW BAGGAGE

If you think your baggage from the past is heavy, try getting married. Marriage can't heal—and often complicates—an over-burdened heart. Suddenly you have your spouse's "bags" to support as well as your own. You and your spouse may have had very different upbringings, which may affect your ideas about parenthood. Once you have a child, the dynamics really get interesting! The demands of child rearing may distract you from—or even numb—the burdens of your baggage, but they are likely to appear again at an inopportune moment. Eventually, our unsettled accounts not only affect us, but our children. When our arms are overloaded with our own bags, they are not free to embrace our children. The weight may only grow heavier for the next generation. In *Something More,* Catherine Marshall Le Sourd identified the "law of generations." "It is the nature of sin to divide, to build walls, resulting in strained relationships or estrangement."[1] If you did not receive this blessing from your parents, it is very possible that they did not receive it from their parents either. It can be very enlightening to explore your parents' relationship with your grandparents, and so on, to uncover patterns that may be three or four generations in the making.

CHILDREN HAVE GOD-GIVEN NEEDS

The way you express love to your children has its roots in both the present and the past. The God-given "hunger" for attention and affection was either *satisfied* or *starved* by those who met your around-the-clock needs. By five years of age, you unconsciously knew the answers to questions like "What is love?" "Who can I trust?" and "How can I get my needs met?" The way you respond to others as an adult reflects what you have come to believe about yourself over the decades since early childhood.

Some of us barely remember last week, much less thirty years ago! We remember only "selected" events that were deeply significant in some way. Why is it that I (Elaine) still remember when my grandmother said she wished I were a television so she could turn me off? Today I understand exactly how she felt, but that memory still "plays back" when I feel inadequate or insecure. Billy Graham's earliest childhood memory of his father was recorded in *Unlocking the Secrets of Your Childhood Memories* by Kevin Lehman and Randy Carlson. "It was in the afternoon. I remember him clapping his hands, opening his arms, calling 'Billy Frank, come to Daddy! C'mon to Daddy, Billy Frank!'"[2] We can appreciate how this exceptional man of God discovered a loving and caring heavenly Father whose arms are opened wide!

THE WAY GOD MEANT IT TO BE

God desires for every child to receive their parents' genuine approval. The first reference to "blessing" was God's first charge to His new creations: "Then God blessed them, and God said to them, 'Be fruitful and multiply'" (Gen. 1:28 NKJV). After the flood destroyed the entire creation, God blessed Noah and his children in the same way: "Be fruitful and multiply, fill the earth" (Gen. 9:1 NKJV). Later, Abram received a more extensive blessing that included all of us. "In you all the families of the earth shall be blessed" (Gen. 12:3 NKJV). This promise was a crown over all the others because it pointed to the coming of Jesus Christ, the greatest blessing the world ever received. Generation after generation, an expectant vision was passed from parent to child. The Old Testament blessing demonstrated extreme confidence in God. Knowing they would not live to see it, parents verbalized the future of their children and grandchildren.

Jesus Loves the Little Children

> Some people brought their children to Jesus so that he could bless them by placing his hands on them. But his disciples told the people to stop bothering him. When Jesus saw this, he became angry and said, "Let the children come to me! Don't try to stop them. People who are like these little children belong to the kingdom of God. I promise you that you cannot get into God's kingdom, unless you accept it the way a child does." Then Jesus took the children in his arms and blessed them by placing his hands on them. (Mark 10:13–16 CEV)

Jesus modeled God's intention for blessing children. The children who were brought to him were not old enough to be taught, yet their parents valued them enough to believe that Christ's blessing was important. Jesus was displeased that the disciples discouraged children from approaching Him. He not only encouraged, but ordered that time be set aside for them. No adult agenda—even "ministry"—was too important to neglect the little ones. Picture Jesus stopping everything to gather the littlest ones onto His lap, then listening to their giggles and questions, then blessing them with His tender words and gentle touch. God calls us to demonstrate that same pattern for our children.

Modeling Jesus' Blessing
Open hearts are demonstrated through time. There is a theory

going around that only the quality of our time counts. Try explaining that to youngsters! In *Point Man,* Steve Farrar wrote, "Quality time comes at the most unusual moments. You never know when it will happen. It usually makes an appearance someplace in the realm of *quantity* time" (emphasis added).[3] Children need our prime time, not just our leftovers. How approachable are you? We never know what small thing in our eyes will be remembered or how it will impact our child. A successful attorney said, "The greatest gift I ever received was a gift I got for Christmas when my dad gave me a small box. Inside was a note saying, 'Son, this year I will give you 365 hours—an hour every day after dinner. It's yours. We'll talk about what you want to talk about. We'll go where you want to go, play what you want to play. It will be your hour!' My dad not only kept his promise, but every year he renewed it—and it's the greatest gift I ever had in my life. I am the result of my father's time."[4]

Open ears are demonstrated through attention. How do you feel when you talk to someone whose mind is miles away, whose gaze is over your shoulder, rather than into your eyes? When parents are tired from long hours and late nights, it is easy to become insensitive to our children. A three-year-old cannot reason that Mommy has a headache or Daddy is upset over a business loss. Wondering why they can't get through, they may experiment with negative means of gaining our attention. Others withdraw into a private world. Literally getting down on your knees and establishing eye contact with your child reassures them that you are *attempting* to understand their message. Your undivided attention will allow you to interpret much more than they express with their limited vocabulary!

Open arms are demonstrated by affection. Some of you never heard the words "I love you" or received hugs conveying acceptance. Others endured the inappropriate advances of a relative or friend. Both may have difficulty showing simple acts of tenderness toward others. Children need to know that being with Mom and Dad is the safest place on earth. If this pattern is developed during the early years, parents will continue to be a safe harbor for children physically, emotionally, and spiritually during the turbulent adolescent years. Physical affection includes *appropriate touch*—gentle pats, hugs, kisses, even "horseplay." Mark Twain once said, "I can live two months on a good compliment." However, kids are not mind readers. They should never leave the house or go to bed without hearing sincere expressions of devotion to them.

Blessing the "Unblessed"

Not everyone is "blessed" by their earthly parents. Pride, excessive self-indulgence, and depravity drive some adults to neglect or mistreat innocent children. God left a promise for you if this happened to you: "Can a woman forget her nursing child, and not have compassion on the son of her womb? Surely they may forget, yet I will not forget you" (Isa. 49:15 NKJV). Even if your earthly parents somehow defaulted on their parental responsibility, you can be assured that your heavenly parentage remains secure. In the culture of Paul's day, a natural child could be disowned, but an adopted child could never be denied. Romans 8:15–17 promises, "You did not receive the spirit of bondage again to fear, but you received the Spirit of adoption by whom we cry out, 'Abba, Father.' [intimate, like Daddy] The Spirit Himself bears witness with our spirit that we are children of God, and if children, then heirs" (NKJV). God acknowledges that ultimately He will bring both comfort and justice for His children who have been troubled, crushed, or made brokenhearted by their earthly parents.

UNPACKING YOUR UNNEEDED LUGGAGE

Elaine and I are very different in the way we deal with luggage when we return from a trip. Even if it is 3:00 A.M., I have to unload everything and put it away. She doesn't mind unpacking a little at a time over several days. Most of us would rather throw the bags in the closet and forget about them! The problem with dirty laundry is similar to unresolved issues—both begin to "stink" if they're postponed too long. Everyone deals with disturbing experiences differently. Some deny them. Some discount them. Some are tormented over them. Regardless of your approach, you will not be rid of them until you put them away.

Unlock Each Bag with Truth

In *The Bondage Breaker,* Neil T. Anderson wrote that most false beliefs are formed during the developmental years of childhood. He states that "the power of Satan is in presenting the lie. The power of the believer is in knowing the truth."[5] Jesus provided the same path to insight and healing: "And you shall know the truth, and the truth shall make you free" (John 8:32 NKJV). Discovering and applying God's Word to hurtful experiences is like medicine used on a cut. It stings at first, then penetrates, and after the infection is killed, the pain begins to subside. Hebrews 4:12 describes the insight gained from God's Word as living, active, sharp, piercing, and able to judge everything—even memories carefully buried or hidden for many years. Begin to replace the old "tapes" with God's truth from Scripture: "You'll never change." ("He who has begun a good work in you will complete it until the day of Jesus Christ" Phil. 1:6 [NKJV]). "You'll never amount to anything." ("For I know the thoughts that I think toward you . . . thoughts of peace and not of evil, to give you a future and a hope" Jer. 29:11 [NKJV]). "No one will ever love you." ("How great is the love the Father has lavished on us, that we should be called children of God! And that is what we are!" 1 John 3:1 [NIV]). Just as lies can hold you captive, God's truth will finally liberate you to move forward in freedom.

Cast Off Each Bag with Forgiveness

Those who have been mistreated or abused are ultimately left to make sense of the past, grieve the loss, and get on with life. Some spend hours imagining how God will annihilate the "offender." If nothing happens, they may lose hope. They may decide God doesn't care, or even exist. Eventually, every wounded person reaches the same crisis point. The most difficult step for a "victim" or "survivor" is crossing the giant chasm called *forgiveness*. C. S. Lewis said, "Everyone claims that forgiveness is a wonderful idea until they have something to forgive. Our judicial hearts tend to rate insults by how unforgivable they are."[6] A search of Scripture won't turn up any transgression beyond God's forgiveness.

How happy and humbled we are to realize that our debts to God have been paid in full by the extravagant sacrifice of Jesus Christ! He didn't wait until we felt bad enough or tried to pay Him back, or deserved it. He didn't drive us to repentance, but drew us by persistently loving us. We tend to excuse and downplay our own sins against God as "mistakes" or "slipups." We too easily forget the extreme measures God took to release us and wipe away our offenses toward Him. We also exaggerate the smallest insults from others, elevating them as equal with sinning against God Himself. And how do we respond to them? *How can I forgive?* The answer is tough, but clear. We have no choice in the matter.

God commands us to release our enemies to His justice if we ever hope to be released from our own pain. That seems so backward in a dog-eat-dog, eye-for-an-eye world, but God's ways are often opposite of human reasoning. He tells us to pray for God to forgive them, to speak well of them, and to *actively do good* to them. No wonder God calls reconciliation a *ministry*—only He could empower us for such a supernatural response! If the cost of forgiveness seems too high, keep in mind that the cost of unforgiveness is even higher. Vindictiveness—not the person who hurt you—will keep you tied to the past. Your children will pick up on the way you respond to relationship problems if you let *who you are* be defined by who has injured you.

PACKING FOR A NEW DESTINATION

Early one fall, we planned a long weekend in the Florida Keys. It is easier to pack for the beach than some vacations—swimsuits and sunscreen don't take up much room! When we got to the airport, we were shocked to learn that our flight had been canceled. A hurricane was heading in the direction of our destination! We called our travel agent in a panic, and she offered to arrange another travel package—in Chicago. Four hours later, we returned to the airport with suitcases stuffed with jeans and sweaters. It wasn't the trip we had planned to take, but ended up being one of the best times we ever spent together!

You cannot erase the past, but you don't have to stay there. Forgiveness is not ignoring conflict, excusing immorality, or tolerating continuing abuse. It is not immediate or clean-cut. Facing painful events from the past may bring forward strong emotions of grief, fear, anger, or guilt. Acknowledging them and allowing them to run their course is half the journey. The rest of the pilgrimage is looking toward the future with new eyes.

How Can I Forget?

When we fully release our past to God, He will begin the process of restoring our future. Look how close "forgive" and "forget" are. *To forgive* is a gift only God can enable us to give. *To forget* is a gift only God can enable us to receive. "Remembering to forget" may be a slow process. Beware of returning to the past. In *Unlocking the Secrets of Your Childhood Memories*, Lehman and Carlson said, "A lot of folks like to dig around in their past and find excuses for their present behavior."[7] A friend shared her method for dealing with recurring memories that she has already "sent home" to God. As a little girl, she witnessed her mother being severely beaten by her father. Years later, while praying with a group of women, she pictured Jesus sitting with her on the stairs. She imagined Him holding her hand and comforting her mother, whom He had clothed with clean robes. Now when the memory replays, she views it differently.

Our tainted outlook on life is reflected by our tendency to read the Ten Commandments in the negative. It is easy to focus on the consequences of the past, when we read that our baggage was passed down to us from previous generations. "For I, the LORD your God, am a jealous God, visiting the iniquity of the fathers on the children to the third and fourth generations of those who hate Me" (Ex. 20:5 NKJV). We may forget that the opposite is true in an even greater sense. "Therefore know that the LORD your God, He is God, the faithful God who keeps covenant and mercy for a thousand generations with those who love Him and keep His commandments" (Deut. 7:9 NKJV).

It is time for the years of destruction and brokenness to be restored. We are no longer slaves to the past, so there is nothing in the future to fear. God says we were chosen to be His children. We have been permanently adopted as sons and daughters, making intimacy with our heavenly "Abba" a reality. He has reserved the best blessings for His children, and has great plans for us *today*. Paul gave our final marching orders: "But one thing I do: Forgetting what is behind and straining toward what is ahead, I press on toward the goal to win the prize for which God has called me heavenward in Christ Jesus" (Phil. 3:13–14 NIV). Don't give up! God is the perfect parent and He will build a new heritage for future generations of your family.

A parent's prayer . . . Lord, why am I so slow to learn? You are beginning to reveal some of the patterns in my life that are so entrenched that I haven't even recognized them. Why do I behave the way I do, think the way I do? Is it really all for the purpose of getting acceptance?

I want to move ahead, yet I am beginning to realize that I must turn around and look my past in the face. Lord, I confess my sin of manipulating everyone around me (especially my family) to get what I want. Sometimes what I want isn't even so bad, its how I seek to get it and who I seek to get it from. Jesus, I am turning away from my attitudes and schemes to receive Your forgiveness and the only love that can satisfy my needs. Oh God, help them and help me. Let them develop a healthy knowledge of Your endless, boundless love. By Your grace, let me show them the way, even as I stumble.

DISCUSSION QUESTIONS

1. Which of your childhood experiences do you hope to duplicate with your children? Which experiences do you hope to avoid?

2. What "bags" have you carried into your marriage and parenting?

3. What is your most positive childhood memory? Most negative? Most embarrassing? Think about it for a few minutes and then share each one.

4. Of all the millions of tapes in your brain, why do you think you still remember the ones you do?

5. How did your parents give you the blessings of time, attention, and affection?

6. Which blessing (time, attention, affection) does your child need most from you today? (If you have more than one child, answer the question individually for each child.)

7. Complete these statements:
   I know my parents love(d) me because ...
   Sometimes I question(ed) my parents' love for me because ...

Part Two:

Drafting Your Plan

When we see a handcrafted cabinet we know it was made by a cabinetmaker. We have no difficulty at all in assuming this even though we did not see it made. Yet when we look up into the vastness of the universe and see stars moving in orderly relationship in vast interstellar space, we speak vaguely about chance and accident. If the universe originated randomly rather than by design, then nothing in this universe or in our lives has lasting purpose. If there is no Creator, no heavenly Father with the power or will to influence our lives, how can we hope to shape the lives of our children?

Halley's Comet, a ball of ice and dust orbiting the sun, can be seen from the earth approximately once every seventy-six years. The path of the comet extends from near the sun to beyond the planet Neptune. Chinese astronomers first recorded the appearance of a "broom star" in 239 B.C. It was named for English astronomer Edmund Halley who first demonstrated that comets revolved in elliptical orbits around the sun. He also accurately predicted that the comet would return in 1758. For the last two decades, space probes have been studying and photographing Halley's comet on its passes near the earth. Does Halley's Comet return by accident or design? Scripture says there is both a plan and a Master Architect—and that God's marvelous, orderly creation makes His invisible qualities clear even to people who haven't ever heard of Him (Rom. 1:19–20). Psalm 104 assures us that God is still the ruler over all of His creation.

Just as He sustains the order of the stars and planets, God will never walk away from His ultimate creation. He is working behind the scenes to execute a well-orchestrated plan for each one of us! Shape another generation? Significantly influence values? More than two hundred verses from the Bible about parenting shout "Yes!" The shaping of a generation begins with parents who take the time to design a well-organized, methodical plan for character building. God has given us the pattern, and we are called to be apprentices under His watchful supervision. But our window of opportunity is fleeting. Like Halley's Comet, the chance comes once for each generation, but God has a definite design in mind for your unique child. The next four chapters will take you from the drafting table to the construction site—so grab a pencil and a hard hat and let's get started!

5 ∤ Parenting by Chance or Design?

"And the Child grew and became strong in spirit, filled with wisdom; and the grace of God was upon Him."
—*Luke 2:40* NKJV

One night a couple of prowlers broke into a department store. They successfully entered the store, stayed long enough to finish what they came to do, and escaped unnoticed. What is unusual about this story is that these fellows took absolutely nothing. No items were removed and no merchandise was destroyed. Instead, these clever pranksters changed the price tags on all the merchandise! They stuck the tag on a $395.00 camera on a $5.00 box of stationery. A price of $9.95 from a paperback book was placed on an outboard motor and so on. Crazy? Maybe. But the most bizarre part happened the next morning. The store opened as usual. Employees went to work. Customers began to shop—and business carried on as usual for *four hours* before anyone noticed what had happened. Some people got some real bargains, while others got ripped off![1]

The same thing has happened to our culture. Our moral compass has been tampered with. Our conscience has been numbed. What used to have great value—character, faith, service—has been replaced with situation ethics, New Age spirituality, and self-regard. Doesn't anyone notice that the price tags have been switched? Morality is judged according to the changing polls, and a culture that continues with a business-as-usual attitude. Parents who hope to change the direction of the next generation can't afford to be careless and expect their children to adopt a higher standard.

PARENTING BY CHANCE

How many times have you heard parents ask, "Where did we go wrong?" after their son or daughter "blew it" as a teen or young adult? It's easy for outsiders to presume to know the answer. "They didn't spend enough time with their kids," or, "They were too permissive—or too strict!" More often there is no way to project the blame accurately. When it comes to the complexities of building people's lives, parents grope for gauges to measure how they are doing. That may explain our tendency to emphasize performance and achievement, which are usually quantitatively scored. Getting our hands around subjective concepts like ethics, convictions, and ideals is much more difficult.

A Builder's Nightmare

Once a man had a grand idea of building a new home unlike any other in the neighborhood. He purchased a beautiful corner lot with wonderful old trees. He found the builder with the best reputation in the community. He met with the builder to describe all the features he wanted in his new home. At the insistence of the buyer, the builder began construction using a set of blueprints from a house he built years before. Day after day the client came to the construction site to make suggestions about new features he wanted to add and changes he wanted to make to the floor plan and elevation. Finally, the house was completed, but the owner was upset because it didn't turn out as he imagined. The den had too many windows. The roof lines were choppy and asymmetrical. Several other items weren't quite right, especially when he received the closing figures for all the changes. After several months of arguing back and forth, the man took his case to court. In the end, the judge ruled in favor of the builder—because the owner could not produce a set of blueprints for the house he had intended to build.

BENEFITS OF A BLUEPRINT

Few people would seriously consider building a house without a set of blueprints. For a building to be structurally sound and architecturally complete it must be painstakingly designed in advance. All of the elements including the foundation, structure, roof, mechanical systems, doors, and windows must be mapped out in detail. Parents would agree with great conviction that children are more important than houses or material things. We plan their meals, their schedules, their education, and their vacations, but few take the time to literally design a plan for intentional character development. God's Word has given the necessary details and dimensions needed to design a workable plan for building strong lives.

Crystallizes Your Purpose

Watching small children play soccer is really quite comical. Most of the kids don't understand the different positions, so they all huddle together, wildly kicking at the ball, which you can't see because the group moves about like a "herd." Meanwhile, there's at least one child off picking flowers or chasing butterflies instead of tending the goal (not that it matters!). Why? Because little kids don't see that the object of soccer is to score points by kicking the ball away from the huddle, down the field, and into the goal. Parents can also forget that "huddling" with everyone else is not the goal of parenthood. Kicking the ball in the goal for Christians is doing whatever is necessary to develop young champions for Christ.

Helps Children Gain Confidence

Children who know what is expected of them are more secure. Studies have shown that too much freedom can actually stifle exploration and creativity in young children. If they are "clueless" regarding the character qualities expected of them, it is unlikely that those traits will spontaneously appear on their own. When they know what the target is, even young children can display positive attributes after some purposeful building.

Gives Specific Strategy

Most of us could reel off a list of qualities we wish our children possessed. However, definite steps must be "nailed down" to achieve our goals. A contractor cannot simply instruct his crew to build a bathroom without a plan for installing the pipes and fixtures in the proper order and position. Parents cannot expect godly character to spring up magically without an orderly and systematic approach to character building.

Helps Anticipate Obstacles

When General Motors announced the opening of the new Saturn plant in Spring Hill, Tennessee, everyone became curious to see the automobile they were building. Although the first models were sold to the public in 1990, the experts had already been driving disguised test models all over the country. They wanted to get a head start and correct as many problems as possible before the buyer ever got behind the wheel of their product. A definite design keeps us aware of potential pitfalls we are bound to encounter like the influence of media and education on our youngsters.

Keeps Us Accountable

Parents are ultimately accountable to God for our workmanship in our children's lives. A character blueprint provides a concrete reminder of the attributes for which we are aiming. A contractor usually "subs out" tasks to craftsmen skilled in various areas, but each must report back to him. Parents are partners with God as well as extended family, teachers, coaches, and church members who help with the design we've developed, yet the responsibility falls on the shoulders of the parents.

Understanding Your Child's Design

While there are guiding principles for designing a character blueprint, parents are not meant to be mass-manufacturers of perfect little soldiers. We are more like "custom" builders, which requires us to make a careful study of our children. Becoming a student of your child is the first step in the design process. Before you had your child, there were so many things you couldn't wait to know. Is it a boy or girl? Will he be big or little? Will she be blonde, have curly hair, or be bald? Friendly or shy? Compliant or incorrigible? When they finally arrived, you watched and listened and waited for a little person to emerge. What could you know about someone who only ate, slept, cried, and made messy diapers? Month by month, your infant began to stay awake more, and smile, then laugh—and began to interact with you. This is the season when parents and children become strongly attached. How well you know your child doesn't depend on your IQ, social position, or educational background. It depends on how well you are paying attention as you interact with your child each day. A few select volumes have guided us through our parenting years. One is a tattered baby care book that is highlighted, dog-eared, and spotted with pink antibiotic stains from all the times we held a crying baby while searching for confirmation that this, too, was "normal." Bookcases may contain scores of subjects from health care to discipline to sexuality—but are our Bibles as well worn as our pediatric manuals?

Keeping Your Balance

Everything written about Jesus' life from birth to age thirty is recorded in the second chapter of Luke. His parents meticulously followed the Scriptures in their child rearing. Can you imagine being the parents of the only perfect child in history? The worst thing He did was to disappear during a family mission trip. His frantic parents found Him debating and teaching in the synagogue—no wonder it took them three days to find Him! Was He strange? Rebellious? An egghead? On the contrary, Jesus led a well-balanced life as a young man and "continued in subjection to them . . ." In order to understand your child better, you must assess whether you are overemphasizing or neglecting any of the four developmental areas identified in Luke 2:52 (NKJV): "Jesus increased in wisdom and stature, and in favor with God and men." Each of these areas is essential to the development of a complete child.

Intellectual (Jesus Grew in Wisdom)

Every child is born with an individualized timetable for development. Each progresses at their own rate—and most develop within the orderly framework God ordained. One of the most difficult traps for parents to avoid is comparing their child with others their age. Especially from birth to three years of age, there is a wide range of "normal." Some two-year-olds converse like adults, while an equally intelligent child still uses single words. By three, both have usually reached the same milestones—highly verbal preschoolers who are asking constant questions! Parents should provide plenty of creative experiences before the formal school years. Educators recommend that parents who want to prepare their children to be lifelong learners should read to them every day. If you have any concerns about your child's speech, motor, or cognitive (learning) development, never hesitate to question professionals. Assessments and early intervention are available free of charge to *all* infants and toddlers under age three. In addition, your public schools are mandated to provide early childhood services starting at age three, through the IDEA act.[2]

Physical (Jesus Grew in Stature)

The most apparent early milestones are the physical (or motor) accomplishments. Vigilant parents hold their breath until their child sits up, walks, or pedals a tricycle. This area is easy to get out of balance. Unfortunately, our daughters are programmed to follow after the world's standards for beauty. Our sons are pressured to excel in athletics. Parents should do more to encourage strong, healthy, rested bodies. We should spend less of our money and concern on accentuating the latest styles or status labels. We must inspire them to seek after inner beauty and inner strength as well.

Social/Emotional (Jesus Grew in Favor with Men)

Each child is born with a distinct temperament and personality that may be quite different from their parents and siblings. Is your child easily upset or easygoing? A leader or follower? Playful or serious? Experiences outside the home influence emotional and social development. Some children are comfortable around new faces while others cling tightly to their family circle. Your awareness of your child's unique disposition and customary responses will enable you to develop corresponding strengths to offset any weaknesses.

Spiritual (Jesus Grew in Favor with God)

Some parents avoid this area because they are afraid of turning off their children to God. If we do not actively prepare and lead our children spiritually, we are hindering them from reaching their full potential. Children have a fabulous capacity for understanding spiritual concepts even when they are small. The key is to make God an important part of your conversations. They need to see that God truly is a part of everyday life. Parents must practice to make spiritual dialogues feel natural. We will develop this thought more fully in later chapters.

PARENTING BY DESIGN!

Really understanding your wonderfully unique child takes concentrated doses of time. Once you have made a study of your child in the areas mentioned above, there are four more actions to incorporate as you begin designing your character-building blueprint.

Observe Your Child's Actions

Amanda came home crying because someone called her "Mrs. Weirdo." Later, the teacher informed us that "poor little Amanda" spit on him to return the compliment! Like it or not, we are not the only ones observing our children. From their youngest days the world is watching and judging our little ones—not only their appearance, but also their behavior and habits. Do you know how your child behaves when you're not around? This is your chance to be a private eye. Stand outside the door or an open window when your child is playing with a friend or sibling. Ask a teacher for honest, specific feedback—and receive it gratefully. Count it a blessing when you "accidentally" find out what your son or daughter is really up to—that way you can deal with minor character flaws before they become glaring ones.

Join in Your Child's Activities

It's fun to watch a parent who has learned the art of playing imaginatively with a child. As we become more involved in activities *they* enjoy (from rattle shaking to scribbling to Candyland), we will behold the colorful characters God has placed in our care. Whether they are throwing the ball or bathing a baby doll, let your child direct your playtimes together. David has graciously attended tea parties and radio shows with alter ego "Brookie Tyler" and I've endured my quota of insect projects and muddy adventures.

"Watch this!" is a universal characteristic of child's play. Concerts, puppet shows, and skits allow children to "try on" different characters and personalities within the safety of the imagination. Another benefit of playing with your children is rediscovering the carefree kid in yourself!

Chronicle Your Child's Milestones

If you happened to be the sibling who came along close behind a brother or sister, you may have experienced the dismay of searching for childhood pictures of yourself. More than likely, your parents did not purposely neglect snapping photos of you—they were just too busy changing diapers or chasing your sibling to get around to it! Now that we share in this mystical fraternity called parenthood, we understand how quickly the days slip by, with memories etched only in our tired heads—who has time for scrapbooks or journals? As difficult as it is, recording your child's development can become a priceless treasure. Their very own memory book provides a wonderful review of your precious moments together. A parent's spiritual journal gives evidence of God's faithfulness during the fleeting years of childhood. A magnetized pad on the refrigerator may be the best place to record the hilarious things children say—and a "banker's box" for each child is an easy place to keep pictures and scrapbook "stuff" until you can get around to making an album. I (Elaine) used to buy big artist's portfolios every year to keep the pictures the kids painted—someday we'll dig those out and reminisce. Some people even save their children's baby teeth! Our family has shared a lot of laughs watching videos of birthdays, Christmases, programs, and school projects. Our favorite has been the boys' fifth-grade Egypt project with Joel as Queen Hapshetsut and Blake as Dr. Ooleeki hosting "Tomb Improvement." These are jewels that can never be recaptured if we aren't better historians. The Bible shows that God is a chronicler of our days and has several books of remembrance (Mal. 3:16). If He can keep up with His children, we can too!

Treasure Your Child's Days

When our children were preschoolers, we had season passes to a local theme park. For the first few years, they happily climbed in the ball cage, and rode the carousel, the little boats, and the mini roller coaster. As they got older, they began eyeing the "big" rides—but a colorful yardstick let them know they were *too little* to ride them. Year after year, they grew, and gradually were able to ride the *biggest* roller coasters and the *fastest* cars. They would rush past the planes and the little ferris wheel without a thought. We will never forget the sad day when Amanda returned to check out her old favorites and was told she was *too big* to ride them. Why are we in such a hurry to rush through the "golden years" of childhood? If we listened carefully, we might catch ourselves making statements like, "I can't wait until he goes to school," or, "If we can just get her out of diapers," or, "After they get older we can go on vacations." The trouble with looking too far ahead—or behind—is that we miss today. We need to cherish the *present,* despite all its flaws and inconveniences. "So teach us to number our days, That we may gain a heart of wisdom" (Ps. 90:12 NKJV). Only God can help us number our days wisely, for we cannot make one of them come back to us again.

DESIGNING YOUR FAMILY BLUEPRINT

We have built several houses during the last twenty years. They have varied in size and in style and in detail. At one point, we spent over a year designing and building our "dream house," with all the space and features that anyone could ever desire. The setting was idyllic, the interior was beautiful, and the children thrived in our spacious, peaceful haven. Less than two years later, an economic downturn, and a domino effect on a number of business investors, forced us to leave the home we had joked was "the last stop before the cemetery." We moved to an old, unrestored home of half the size yet our children remained carefree and never looked back.

When God confirmed our calling to a vocational ministry, our life-style changed yet again to give us the freedom to respond to His plan. We never anticipated that plan would include living four years in a two-bedroom town house. All three children shared a room, and we worked from an open loft—four long summers with the kids literally beneath our feet. It was a refining experience for us—but our children look back and agree that the years where we had the very least were the best memories they had of their child-hood. It began to sink in that the only "specs" and blueprints we should be concerning ourselves with are those that pertain to the lives of our children. God is not as concerned about the structure you live in as what is happening inside the walls. Parents should not be so worried about giving our children the best of the world, but rather the best of ourselves.

As we are writing this manuscript, we are building a home from a newly designed blueprint. Before it was started, we had only seen it on paper. This time we haven't concentrated so much on the outside features. Instead, we have tried to think of what will be happening inside. We've tried to keep in mind that within six years, all of our children may be gone. Behind every decision are the dreams we still have for wisely investing in our last years together. Our window of opportunity to influence their hearts is flying by much more quickly than we thought. Birth to kinder-garten seemed like an eternity. Elementary school was so pleasant that it should have been suspended in time. Middle school whizzed by so fast we grew dizzy—and high school seems like where *we* should still be! "These are the golden years," means so much more now than ever before. Maybe saving all their baby teeth wasn't such a bad idea after all!

A parent's prayer ... Lord, turn my dreams into plans. You know how I hope the children will grow into mature adults who are strong in character. But sometimes my thoughts and ideas never make it to action. I need to balance being idealistic and practical at the same time. Help me become more intentional and strategic about developing and building character. The only character reference worth imitating is Yours. My own still needs plenty of work. I am most sobered by the thought that my children are watching me and learning from me. Next week we move into a newly built house. As we were walking through it yesterday, I was impressed by the craftsmanship. But I know it all began with the blueprint. As the great Architect, guide me as I pore over the blueprints for my children. Heighten my attention to every detail. The construction of their character will be complete before I know it. Enable me to finish strong.

DISCUSSION QUESTIONS

1. Imagine the days when your children will be old enough to leave home. What character qualities will they need most? Why?

2. How balanced is your emphasis on physical, intellectual, social/emotional, and spiritual development? Which area do you tend to overemphasize? Underemphasize? What steps will you take to bring more balance?

3. Who (or what) was the greatest character shaper in your life? How intentional was their training?

4. What obstacle makes developing an intentional and detailed plan for your child's character difficult? How can that obstacle be overcome?

6 } Partnering with the Architect

*"For we are God's fellow workers
you are . . . God's building."*
—*1 Corinthians 3:9 NKJV*

Before you were even born, God stamped His mark on you and masterfully designed a plan for your life. He intended for your parents to build a foundation that would last you a lifetime. He meant for them to carefully choose the right materials and prepare you for your life calling. Others came along to help with the construction until you became an adult. Looking at yourself as a "building," how have you held up over the years? Can you say that your parents were "expert builders"? And what kind of builder are you prepared to be for your own children? Throughout Scripture building things is compared to building lives—and building lives is the primary aim of parenthood. In Hebrews 11:10, God is called the "architect" and "builder" of "the city which has foundations" (NASB). Christian parents are engaged in God's business. Our high calling is outlined in 1 Corinthians 3:10 (NKJV): "According to the grace of God which was given to me, as a wise master builder I have laid the foundation." God has chosen us to build our children's foundation under His watchful eye. Only God can cause the growth, and we cannot afford to be indifferent about how we build. He doesn't want us to remain as apprentices and He will teach us to be "wise master builders."

COUNTING THE COST

When Jesus was teaching His disciples, He asked them,

Suppose one of you wants to build a tower. What is the first thing you will do? Won't you sit down and figure out how much it will cost and if you have enough money to pay for it? Otherwise, you will start building the tower, but not be able to finish. Then everyone who sees what is happening will laugh at you. They will say, "You started building, but could not finish the job." (Luke 14:28–30 CEV)

Just as parents sit down to figure out how much it will cost to pay for their son's or daughter's college education, we should also calculate the cost of raising our children according to God's design. As you work out the specifications for your blueprint, what sacrifices and investments will be required? Planning, preparation—and plenty of time—are just a few. Who will complete the job? You may need some training to become a skilled "craftsman." Are you willing to pay any price to raise your child in the way you know God desires? Take time to calculate the cost.

LAYING THE PROPER FOUNDATION

Jesus told a parable about two home builders who constructed their houses on different foundations. One chose to build on a rocky hillside. The other chose a soft, sandy beach. An observer might have appraised these homes as equal in quality, but the distinction in the end was the foundation. When the rain and the flood and the wind came, only the house built on the rock was left standing. Like literal foundations, the "inner" person may not be the first thing noticed—but the foundation on which character is built will be revealed by life's inevitable "storms." Many parents attempt to build on foundations like education, family life, church commitment, community service, or the American dream. The Bible says, "No one can lay any foundation other than the one already laid, which is Jesus Christ" (1 Cor. 3:11 NIV). Without this base, it will be extremely difficult to accomplish other character goals. What kind of foundation have you been laying for your children?

THE GOLDEN RULE OF PARENTING

Parents usually think of themselves as child-molders, but it seems God has a more humorous plan in mind. Quite often, He uses our children as parent-molders! They are not as easily fooled as our coworkers or church friends who don't usually see us during our worst moments. Children know us as we really are. They may not understand a lot of things, but they recognize hypocrisy quite easily. In a personal letter to Charles Swindoll, Tim Hansel mentioned a rather extensive Harvard University study conducted within recent years. Their findings surprised even those doing the study. Amid the high-tech sophistication and advanced techniques of our world, the number one way to change lives was through modeling.[1] When it is all said and done, the best way to impact another life is to demonstrate, to practice what one teaches. Thus, we have one of the most important principles of parenting: *You cannot transfer what you do not have.*

Suppose I want to demonstrate love to my children in a very tangible way. I think I'll write a check to my firstborn, Blake, for $1 million. I have no doubt that Blake will be celebrating in a big way! The only trouble is that when he takes my check to the bank, it's going to bounce—*real high.* It's not that my kid isn't worth every penny of it—I simply cannot transfer what I do not have into my bank account. What is the balance in your character bank today? Are you trying to transfer qualities to your children that you don't possess yourself?

The Golden Rule of Parenting works in reverse as well: *You will transfer what you do have.* Our boys recently got their driving permits—now they must practice driving under our supervision for a year before they get their licenses. The downside is that suddenly they notice everything we do when we are driving. There is the four-way stop in our neighborhood that rarely has more than one car at it, so I (David) tend to make what some refer to as a "California stop." Recently, I made one of those stops (more like a slow roll), and Blake asked if that was the way he should stop at that intersection. At that moment, the Golden Rule of Parenting began ringing in my ears! As someone humorously put it, "More things will be caught than taught." Try to remember that when your kids are young—like every time you drive!

PREPARING TO BUILD

A young lumberjack asked a logging crew foreman for a job. The foreman replied, "Well, let's see if you're good enough to work for me." The young man stepped forward and skillfully cut down a large tree. The foreman was impressed and said, "You can start on Monday!" Monday, Tuesday, Wednesday, then Thursday rolled by. On Thursday afternoon the foreman approached the young man. "You can pick up your paycheck on your way out today. We're letting you go because you've fallen behind." The lumberjack cried, "But I'm a hard worker! I arrive first, leave last, and even work through my break times!" The foreman considered the situation for a moment. "Have you been sharpening your ax?" he asked. The young man answered sheepishly, "No. I guess I was working too hard to stop and take the time."[2] The demands of family require large power reserves. If we do not take the time to "sharpen" our private lives, our self-generated energy will be quickly depleted, causing burnout. When we give priority to deepening our relationship with God, we will be more effective workmen.

Inspect Your Foundation

A crack in the foundation can be fatal for any building. What has your life been built upon? Second Corinthians 13:5 says, "Examine yourselves as to whether you are in the faith. Prove yourselves. Do you not know yourselves, that Jesus Christ is in you?—unless indeed you are disqualified" (NKJV). There are really only two categories of foundations on which people build their lives. These categories are exemplified by two men in Scripture—Adam and Jesus. Every human is somehow a descendent of Adam, thus inheriting Adam's "foundation." Through Adam, "sin entered the world, and death through sin, and thus death spread to all men, because all sinned" (Rom. 5:12 NKJV). Four thousand years later, Jesus entered the world, with a foundation like no other human. He was actually God, in the form of a man. His death on the cross paid the debt for all sin. His resurrection from the grave enabled eternal life for all who receive it. "As through one man's offense judgment came to all men, resulting in condemnation, even so through one Man's righteous act the free gift came to all men, resulting in justification of life" (Rom. 5:18 NKJV). Have you accepted the magnificent gift that God has offered?

Your Address Has Changed

Christians are no longer residents of this world, but have become citizens of heaven—where God is carrying out His plans for His kingdom, and where Jesus is preparing a place for them. "For he has rescued us from the dominion of darkness and brought us into the kingdom of the Son he loves, in whom we have redemption, the forgiveness of sins" (Col. 1:13–14 NIV). You not only have a new foundation, you have been made a "living stone," and God's plan is to build Christians into a "spiritual house" (1 Peter 2:4–5).

Your Objective Has Changed

Each person who has received Jesus as their Savior has reached a definite "turning point." When you turn away from life in Adam, and turn *toward* life in Christ, your purpose in life is to carry out the plan of the One who "saved" you. You may have become a Christian recently, or many years ago. Either way, your life may have taken some detours or hit some dead ends since then. As a busy parent, you may have become too preoccupied with building your own little "kingdom" at home, in the marketplace, or even in ministry. When God chose you, He had a different priority in mind: "But seek first the kingdom of God and His righteousness" (Matt. 6:33 NKJV).

Your Job Description Has Changed

The 1991 Movie of the Year was *Driving Miss Daisy*. A headstrong elderly lady (Miss Daisy) was having difficulty facing the fact that she could no longer drive an automobile. Her concerned son hired her a driver and even paid his salary. Unfortunately, she refused to let him drive for her. He sat in the kitchen, day after day, until Miss Daisy finally realized that she was missing out on life by not allowing him to take over. As she swallowed her pride, and let down her guard, she began to develop a deep trust and precious relationship with him until the day she died. Jesus did not come into our lives to keep us company while we sweat and haphazardly "hammer away" at life. He wants to teach us the craft of living well—He wants to take His rightful place as our "driver."

Keeping Divine Appointments

We must prepare for the task of character building, but where do we find the character from which to draw? "Draw near to God and He will draw near to you" (James 4:8 NASB). God has issued a standing invitation to share His presence and receive constant instruction. Just like an appointment with a physician or important business client, Scripture sets the standard for setting aside time to spend alone with God. Just as you would set up a time and place to meet someone you want to get to know better, you may need to take your calendar and literally schedule in "divine appointments." We don't make appointments with God just to check off another thing on our "to do" list. The idea is to set up an environment where God can speak to you and build your character. Those who have tasted the difference that sitting with the Lord over a cup of coffee brings to parenting will work to rearrange schedules to accommodate daily times of refreshment.

Many years ago, there were two men who shared a quality of life that I (David) deeply admired. Both spent time alone with God consistently. Following their example, I began setting aside as much time as possible every morning to read the Bible, memorize Scripture, and journal in a notebook. The difference it made in me caused Elaine to take great pains to protect my "quiet" time (even when she couldn't find the time for herself). The more God corrected and adjusted my thinking, the more I tried to help her find her own time. Nothing we have ever done has so impacted our marriage or approach to parenting as "divine appointments" with God.

God's Schedule Is Open

Before children (B.C.), I (Elaine) spent as much time journaling and studying Scripture as I wanted. When we had three in diapers, they would usually wake up just about the time I got settled! It took persistence to grab time alone, much less time alone with the Lord! During that season of life, I realized that God is available at any moment. Rocking a baby at 4:00 A.M. became an opportunity to pray for each child. Oswald Chambers's devotional book was by the bathtub, a prayer journal waited on the nightstand, and Bible verses stayed by the sink when abbreviated visits with God presented themselves. God anticipates the cries of our hearts and responds to us gladly. He confirms His involvement as our counselor and guide in both small and large details. It doesn't matter as much when, where, or how structured you are, but consistent communication is the key to deepening any relationship.

Start Listening Well

Good communication contains two essential elements: speaking and listening. Not listening is considered pure rudeness, yet stopping to listen to God is the most neglected part of divine appointments. God's primary "voice" is His written Word, the Bible. When we read Scripture, then wait quietly, He has the opportunity to adjust, correct, and refresh our tired minds. The purpose of reading the Bible should not be solely for learning a mass of disconnected information. He wants us to consider the circumstances of our lives in light of His truth. How we handle our children depends on how well we attend to God's Word. Waiting for God to "speak" to you may seem like a mysterious exercise, but He has given us a special interpreter. John 14:26 says, "The Friend, the Holy Spirit whom the Father will send at my request, will make everything plain to you" (The Message).

Start Speaking Honestly

Close friends allow each other the freedom to share their innermost hopes, fears, doubts, even anger. God invites us to talk to Him honestly and openly and conversationally through prayer. Hebrews 4:16 (NASB) reminds us that He is completely approachable—"Let us therefore draw near with confidence to the throne of grace, that we may receive mercy and may find grace to help in time of need." Prayer has many facets including praise, thanksgiving, confession, petition (personal appeals), and intercession (requests for others). One of the most tangible forms of dialoguing with God is journaling—simply writing a note or letter to Him. You can record the greatness of who He is (praise), the faithfulness of what He has done (thanksgiving), disclose what He has revealed (confession, instruction), and bring Him your needs and cares (petition, intercession). Someday, it will be illuminating for you and your children to review how much work God has done in building your life since you transferred it to His foundation.

YOUR FOUNDATION IS SHOWING!

In a very unassuming way, our friend Paul Smith embodies the Golden Rule of Parenting: *You cannot transfer what you do not have—and you will transfer what you do.* It hasn't always been that way. Paul's parents were so consumed with their own unstable lives that they didn't focus on child rearing. As a little boy, he spent most evenings playing on bar stools or shining shoes while his father got drunk—then he began smoking around age eight. From the time he was little, Paul was labeled "trouble." Even at family reunions, relatives didn't want their children to play with him. He was arrested for the first time when he was twelve for stealing cars. Judged incorrigible, he was banished from the state of Ohio until he turned eighteen. Paul was in and out of school until he dropped out his senior year. Why should he stay in school? He never expected to live past twenty-five.

As a young man, his criminal activity escalated to drug dealing and Mafia connections. When he was twenty-five, his "luck" finally ran out. After a stakeout, he was apprehended—but ran over the arresting policeman as he fled. When he was finally taken into custody, he was facing 60–120 years in prison. This was one time, he actually prayed that God would get him out of trouble. Miraculously, his sentence was reduced, then suspended. Evidently, he wasn't the only one praying! Despite their abusive background, his older sister had become a Christian. She began visiting him more often, and would encourage him rather than condemning his life-style. She was the one he trusted several months later, when he exploded with waves of grief during an unexplained panic attack in a bar. He knew he couldn't go on like this any longer. His corrupt life was affecting him physically and emotionally. Because of his sister's concern, he agreed to meet with her pastor, who offered him something he couldn't refuse—if Paul would completely give his life to God for thirty days, the pastor promised that no one would ever bother him again if he wasn't a changed man within a month. He didn't refuse, though he didn't have much hope that he would ever change. He was at the church every time the doors were open while he waited out his thirty days.

Some of the changes were instantaneous. His neck, which he could not turn after months of severe pain, was healed. Suddenly Paul was thrust into a new life and a new job. He had never held an honest job before! Some of the changes were gradual. He never stole or sold drugs again, but sometimes reverted to behaviors that had been "branded" into his character for decades. Other weaknesses remained private strongholds for years, until God brought complete healing. An immediate sign of encouragement was an "angel" from God named Cindy. Somehow she discerned the hand of God on Paul's life, and they were married three months later.

Their upbringings were poles apart, yet Cindy had a vision for helping him change the future! Before too long they had two sons of their own. Paul didn't want them to grow up as he had. He bought a business, and began working late hours, then weekends, then Sundays—until one day it finally hit him. He wanted his boys to know that he loved them. He wanted to be around to teach them right from wrong. He didn't want to risk losing them. So he literally walked away from his partnership, and went home to start a new heritage. The first two rules he implemented were: Saturdays are for family. Sundays are for God.

Over the years, Paul and Cindy have invested great amounts of time and energy into loving and training their boys. Paul has owned a thriving car repair business for many years, but has remained committed to closing the shop on weekends—period. Whether the guys went bowling or fishing, rode dirt bikes or attended concerts, they always set aside the day to play every Saturday. Sundays were reserved for church and related activities with Christian friends. The consistency of their mom and their father's growing faith were so contagious that both boys became Christians at the young age of five.

It is a wondrous mystery how God drew Paul Jr. and Brian to Himself through two related events that happened four years apart. Cindy led Paul Jr. to Christ at his insistence after the critical illness of his grandfather. Four years later, Brian declared that he needed to be saved soon after his grandfather's funeral. How odd—yet how like God, that the grandfather who had left no legacy of faith for his own children was actually the catalyst for his grandsons to find God for themselves!

When we first met the Smiths, we were struck by Paul's smile, which could melt a glacier. His sparkling eyes held no trace of the pain from his past. Paul Jr. was in college and had just married a fine Christian girl—a pastor's daughter. Sixteen-year-old Brian was in high school—all boy, yet already a true servant and leader among his peers. Before his junior year Brian was elected president of the Fellowship of Christian Athletes—just like his brother, four years before. One Sunday he placed a prayer request in the offering basket. It regarded being the right kind of example for his buddies at school. A few days later, Cindy called, "I love you"—as always—when he left the house to go to his church community group; but Brian never arrived, because his car was hit head-on not far from their home.

Brian never awakened again before slipping away to Jesus. Surrounded by hundreds of adults and young people whom the family had quietly influenced, Paul and Cindy responded with supernatural faith in God's purposes. Brian's prayer to be a good example was answered in an unexpected way. His funeral was both heart-wrenching and celebratory. Approximately one thousand students and adults heard the gospel message and the testimony of Brian's love for his Lord.

The glory—despite all the pain—is not in the dramatic reformation of a wayward boy, or the early conversion of his two sons. The glory that belongs to God is how He orchestrated the transformation of an entire family heritage. No doubt you will feel inadequate in one way or another to influence your child's life. God yearns for you to sincerely make Him your foundation, so you can begin building your own child's character. He will lead you to rich mines of peace and strength—and will shape the most unlikely worker into a master builder. Have you counted the cost? Inspected your foundation? Your building cannot fail when you're partnering with the Architect!

> Your foundations I will lay in sapphires.
> Moreover, I will make your battlements of rubies,
> And your gates of crystal,
> And your entire wall of precious stones.
> And all your sons will be taught of the LORD;
> And the well-being of your sons will be great. (Isa. 54:11–13 NASB)

A parent's prayer . . . Father, I am sobered by the task of raising champions for You. I am usually more focused on them becoming champions in this world. I am humbled (and grateful) to be Your chosen instrument. Sometimes I feel so overwhelmed with all of the demands of my life that I don't care to count the cost of parenting well. I am so thankful that You have given us The Rock (Jesus) to build our lives on. I know how much I need You, but I forget how much my children's faith depends on my continued spiritual growth. Renew my discipline of meeting with You—not out of obligation, but out of necessity and desire. Allow me to come to you like Your child, so I will know how to father my children. Today, I present a fearful question for You. Exactly what am I transferring to the chil-

dren? I need to know, since the Golden Rule of parenting is already in effect.

DISCUSSION QUESTIONS

1. Which character traits will be easiest for you to pass on to your children? What makes you believe this?

2. Which character traits will be most challenging for you to pass on to your children? Why?

3. How do you to find time to be alone with God? What keeps you from regular divine appointments with Him?

4. Try to trace how God's hand has been orchestrating change in your own character and in the character of your children.

5. If someone asked your children about your "foundation," what would they say?

7 } Creating a Grand Design

"Let our sons in their youth be as grown-up plants,
And our daughters as corner pillars fashioned
as for a palace."
—Psalm 144:12 NASB

For many years, I (David) was a commercial real estate developer. During the 1970s and early 1980s in Houston, Texas, oil companies experienced tremendous growth and profitability. During that time, office building developers known as "merchant builders" made a lot of money. Merchant builders built structures to sell, rather than to own and rent out themselves. Unfortunately, that proved costly for several oil companies. The builders knew they wouldn't own the buildings for the long term, so they often slipped in materials of cheaper quality. The buildings appeared to be durable, high-quality facilities on the outside; however, the merchant builders typically used lower-grade heating and air-conditioning systems that normally break down within five years. They installed glass windows that weren't up to standard efficiency ratings. In the end, the companies that bought these buildings for high prices at the top of the market became losers in more than one way. We need to ask ourselves if we are willing to settle for being merchant builders in our children's lives.

Can we afford to take shortcuts in the foundation and building of their character? We may feel we can get by with a minimum amount of energy and that with the help of grandparents, the church, and school our kids will get by okay. Besides, when we look at their innocent faces (as they sleep!) we can't imagine their lives falling apart years down the road. The danger in ignoring the need to be careful builders is like the product of the merchant builders. On the surface, children may appear to be functioning well for a while, but eventually the effect of lower-quality "materials" and lax attention to detail will surface. Will we set ourselves up for those despairing words, "Where did we go wrong?" As we get into the actual design of the blueprint, we have several choices to make.

DRAFTING YOUR CHARACTER BLUEPRINT

As you set out to create and implement your plan, it would be ideal to take time to get away with your spouse. If you are a single parent, try to enlist a family member or friend for a block of time to brainstorm and devise your strategy. Allow time to pray together and read Scripture before completing the actual design. (After developing the first draft, aim for a one-day retreat each year to update and reevaluate your plan.) Initially, you should individually rank the top ten qualities that you believe your child will need for adolescence and adulthood, and record them on your paper. We used a simple stick figure (see reproducible sample in Appendix A) to record our character qualities. Next, compare notes and discuss why you ranked your set of attributes in their particular order. That should provide hours of healthy debate!

There has been a lot of press both locally and nationally about teaching values to children. Everyone wants to raise respectful, responsible, law-abiding young people. What never seems to be resolved is whose values will be taught. A few years ago, our local newspaper donated $750,000 to create a character-development program for the schools. Readers identified a list of qualities describing a model citizen. We were interested to note that many

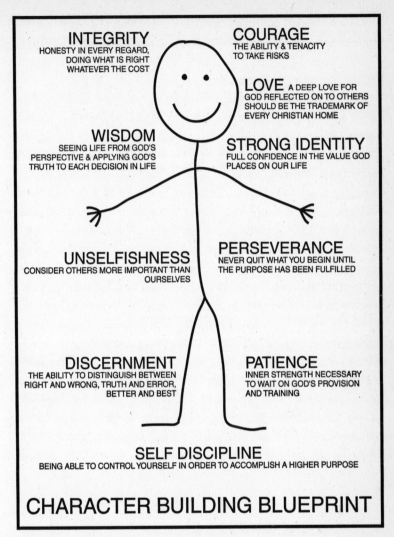

INTEGRITY
HONESTY IN EVERY REGARD,
DOING WHAT IS RIGHT
WHATEVER THE COST

COURAGE
THE ABILITY & TENACITY
TO TAKE RISKS

LOVE A DEEP LOVE FOR
GOD REFLECTED ON TO OTHERS
SHOULD BE THE TRADEMARK OF
EVERY CHRISTIAN HOME

WISDOM
SEEING LIFE FROM GOD'S
PERSPECTIVE & APPLYING GOD'S
TRUTH TO EACH DECISION IN LIFE

STRONG IDENTITY
FULL CONFIDENCE IN THE VALUE GOD
PLACES ON OUR LIFE

UNSELFISHNESS
CONSIDER OTHERS MORE IMPORTANT THAN
OURSELVES

PERSEVERANCE
NEVER QUIT WHAT YOU BEGIN UNTIL
THE PURPOSE HAS BEEN FULFILLED

DISCERNMENT
THE ABILITY TO DISTINGUISH BETWEEN
RIGHT AND WRONG, TRUTH AND ERROR,
BETTER AND BEST

PATIENCE
INNER STRENGTH NECESSARY
TO WAIT ON GOD'S PROVISION
AND TRAINING

SELF DISCIPLINE
BEING ABLE TO CONTROL YOURSELF IN ORDER TO ACCOMPLISH A HIGHER PURPOSE

CHARACTER BUILDING BLUEPRINT

of those traits were on the blueprint we had designed for our children—attributes like honesty, courage, and self-discipline. Great debate arose because the goals started sounding more like religious instruction than character development. Observing this exercise in our community made us wonder about the difference between shaping good citizens and building godly character. Our strategy actually solidified when we finally realized that the essential difference in our case is the source of those same character qualities.

Good Citizen or Godly Person?

A good citizen boasts in his wisdom, strength, and achievements while a godly person gives credit to God for what He has enabled him to accomplish. A good citizen measures herself by others, while a godly person measures herself by God. As we went back to our original blueprint and looked through Scripture, we could see that the difference between raising a moral citizen and a committed Christian has its roots in a parent's convictions and preferences. Convictions are values that withstand time, tyranny, or even death. Preferences are values we prefer until someone changes our mind, disagrees, or threatens our well-being. That brings us to the need to determine our standard for the values we will teach. In *Right from Wrong*, Josh McDowell asserts that *truth* is defined as "fidelity to an original or standard."[1] God's nature defines truth—He is our ideal. From that perspective, it doesn't matter what we think is right or wrong, but what God thinks based on His character. A new parenting principle began to emerge: *God's attributes are the standard for our character building.* Although our list has grown and changed for each of our children, now we revise it by defining each character quality according to the Scripture that identifies it as a corresponding attribute of God.

CHOOSING THE BEST MATERIALS

The "Master Builders Construction List" found in 1 Corinthians 3 specifies distinct differences in the building materials available to us: "Now if anyone builds on this foundation with gold, silver, precious stones, wood, hay, straw, each one's work will become *manifest*; for the Day will declare it" (v. 12–13 NKJV). Consider the articles listed. Gold, silver, and precious stones are not easily acquired because they must be extracted from deep within the earth. They must also be shaped and refined before they become useful. Because of their lasting value, prospectors will go to great lengths to find them. On the other hand, wood, hay, and straw are abundant and inexpensive, and readily available on the earth's surface. They can be gathered quickly but also wither, burn up, or blow away easily. God says each builder's work will ultimately be displayed and tested and tried for its true value: "It will be revealed by fire; and the fire will test each one's work" (1 Cor. 3:13 NKJV). Gold, silver, and precious stones will withstand the refiner's fire and emerge without impurity. Jesus told many more stories about building things. Among them is the parable of the rich man who determined to build himself bigger barns to hold all his crops, only to die the very night he made the decision. (Luke 12:16–21). He had centered his life around temporary things that only benefited himself, and his choice proved to be fatal. Will you take the necessary steps to choose the best materials to erect a truly magnificent structure?

THE "RIGHT STUFF"

Strong Identity—We want our children to be secure in their self-worth because God is our Father.

> Yet to all who received him, to those who believed in his name, he gave the right to become children of God—children born not of natural descent, nor of human decision or a husband's will, but born of God. (John 1:12–13 NIV)

Full confidence in the value God places on our lives correctly defines the concept that secularists have coined "self esteem." It is not the discovery of "who I am" but the discovery of "whose I am." Our children will not have to be taught to love themselves if they are taught how loved they are by their parents and by God. They will need to know from both parents that there is nothing they can do to make you love them any more—and there is nothing they can do to make you love them any less. Preschoolers need to see that it's great to be a boy—or great to be a girl—in order to identify strongly with their own gender. They need to observe parents communicating the value of all people, regardless of race, religion, or social standing. Our prayer is that they will be comfortable enough to dine in a palace or a "pigpen" with equal grace.

Teachability—We want our children to be teachable in every area of life because Jesus is our Teacher.

> Take my yoke upon you and learn from me, for I am gentle and humble in heart, and you will find rest for your souls. (Matt. 11:29 NIV)

The desire to learn and improve and to graciously receive instruction is a prerequisite for further character building. A teachable heart should be emphasized before the first birthday. It will be needed to learn to feed and dress himself, to cross the street, to play a sport, and to learn in school. A teachable heart will also guard against the pride and arrogance that characterize this generation. Teachability is best learned from a consistent, compassionate, and courteous tutor who continues to grow as both scholar and student.

Self-Discipline—We want our children to diligently train themselves for godliness (1 Tim. 4:7) because God is the Perfecter of our faith.

> Let us fix our eyes on Jesus, the author and perfecter of our faith, who for the joy set before him endured the cross, scorning its shame, and sat down at the right hand of the throne of God. (Heb. 12:2 NIV)

The ability to govern yourself in order to accomplish a higher purpose includes the capacity to control your actions, words, and thoughts. Paul instructed young Timothy about diligence—the faithful application of effort, speed, and eagerness to do one's work. Training your children at a young age to take responsibility for their bodies, their behavior, their minds, their money—and so on—will give them an added advantage as they pursue new endeavors throughout their lives.

Wisdom—We want our children to be wise because God is all-knowing.

My purpose is that they may be encouraged in heart and united in love, so that they may have the full riches of complete understanding, in order that they may know the mystery of God, namely, Christ, in whom are hidden all the treasures of wisdom and knowledge. (Col. 2:2–3 NIV)

According to the book of Proverbs, the capacity to view life from God's perspective and to apply God's truth to each decision in life begins with a genuine awe and respect for God. It is also said to be the direct result of a father's instruction and a mother's teaching. A wise person finds practical application for God's truth and maintains an eternal perspective on life. We must teach our children how to apply the wealth of truth found in Scripture to prepare them to walk judiciously through their adolescence and adulthood.

Integrity—We want our children to display integrity because God is Truth.

I am the way, and the truth, and the life; no one comes to the Father, but through Me. (John 14:6 NASB)

Integrity is "built in" best by someone with plenty of experience in applying it. Unfortunately, our children have very few strong role models in this area. A completely honest person with ethical "muscle" is rare—even among professing Christians. Our children will need to stand out among nonbelievers, who are already distrustful of a compromising Christian community. Wouldn't it be nice to be able to insert your son's or daughter's name in place of Job's? "Have you considered My servant _____? For there is no one like him [or her] on the earth, a blameless and upright man, fearing God and turning away from evil" (Job 1:8 NASB).

Discernment—We want our children to have good judgment because God is the Judge of the earth.

> He commanded us to preach to the people and to testify that he [Jesus Christ] is the one whom God appointed as judge of the living and the dead. (Acts 10:42 NIV)

The perceptiveness to distinguish between right and wrong is one of the first things children need to learn. As they enter school, they must be instructed to recognize the subtle differences that often exist between truth and error. As they make more choices about their lives, they must gain a sense of the difference between better and *best*. This spiritual "sixth sense" is a product of the wisdom and knowledge that can only be received by special request from God. If we do not train them to reason judiciously for themselves, how will they avoid second best, deception—or evil—in the days ahead?

Courage—We want our children to have courage because God is omnipotent (all-powerful).

> For with God nothing will be impossible. (Luke 1:37 NKJV)

The ability and confidence to take risks also requires the tenacity to fall short of a goal and try again. Courage means having the grit to stand alone for personal convictions, regardless of what others think. It will be the "glue" that keeps them clinging to God during a moment when all seems lost. The assurance that God is sovereign and that nothing can thwart His plans is the foundation on which a valiant heart can be perfected to withstand the most difficult circumstances life presents.

Perseverance—We want our children to persevere because God is the overcoming One.

> I have told you these things, so that in me you may have peace. In this world you will have trouble. But take heart! I have overcome the world. (John 16:33 NIV)

Perseverance is the predetermined decision never to quit what is begun until its purpose has been fulfilled. This quality begins by requiring our children to finish what they start—from art projects to household tasks, to a full season of a sport they "hate." Steadfastness and persistence will be needed when our children meet up with overwhelming trials and challenges. A therapist used to tell Amanda that "Can't" never did anything—and instead, she should determine "that's hard for me but I will keep trying." A strong faith and hope in God will help our children be "more than conquerors" who never give up on life (Rom. 8:37 NIV).

Patience—We want our children to wait on God because He is Jehovah Jireh (our Provider).

> Abraham looked up and there in a thicket he saw a ram caught by its horns. He went over and took the ram and sacrificed it as a burnt offering instead of his son. So Abraham called that place The LORD Will Provide. (Gen. 22:13–14 NIV)

We live in a time when people expect to have everything—right now. Delayed gratification is a foreign concept. The best things in life often require a waiting period. So do the worst things. Sometimes God postpones the blessings we *feel* we deserve. Sometimes He tests our determination to trust in His provision. And sometimes He allows us to reach the end of ourselves before resolving negative circumstances. These lessons begin early and continue throughout life. Even toddlers must learn to wait a moment longer for what they desire. Children must be taught that saving money yields greater dividends than spending it all. Later, it will be easier to accept that with God, time is on our side—for ultimately, He will shed light on, bring justice to, and provide for every situation in our lives.

Forbearance—We want our children to demonstrate forbearance with others because God is patient.

And be kind to one another, tenderhearted, forgiving one another, just as God in Christ forgave you also. (Eph. 4:32 NKJV)

Another aspect of patience is to endure the weaknesses and peculiarities of others—annoying siblings, unreasonable teachers, irrational employers, and discouraging cynics, to name a few. Children need daily doses of forbearance when receiving advice, completing tasks, and bearing trials without grumbling (Phil. 2:14). Forbearance does not mean refusing to take a stand on morality or injustice, but aiming to live peaceably among all kinds of people. Forgiveness is one of the noblest dimensions of forbearance, and one of the most important to model for our children.

Servanthood—We want our children to be selfless because Jesus was a Servant.

Whoever wishes to be first among you shall be your slave; just as the Son of Man did not come to be served, but to serve, and to give His life a ransom for many. (Matt. 20:27–28 NASB)

The characteristic of putting others first goes directly against the tide in our culture. Everyone must eventually wake up to the fact that the world does not revolve around ME. Children must learn that they do not have to be the center of the universe—or the center of attention—to be fulfilled in life. They must *practice* sharing, taking turns, giving anonymously, and participating in behind-the-scenes acts of kindness. These experiences plant seeds that grow up to find great joy in serving others without the need for recognition or reward.

Love—We want our children to show love because God is Love.

This is love: not that we loved God, but that he loved us and sent his Son as an atoning sacrifice for our sins. (1 John 4:10 NIV)

Jesus summed up the law and prophets with one word—*love* (Mark 12:29–31). Why is the treasure called love so elusive for so many people? Perhaps it is because parents fail to teach their children that genuine love has its source in God alone. From a very young age, most children tease and dissolve one another's self-esteem with insults and put-downs. Parents who do not stop children from making fun of others who are "different" or purposely excluding others from their "inner circle" are training them to judge the value of others. If your own child is ignored or rejected, you must help their broken hearts find the fortress of God's (and your) love. Continue to create an atmosphere of Jesus-based (rather than performance-based) acceptance, so that they will develop the deep compassion to extend love to someone else who longs for this ultimate gift.

DEVELOPING YOUR CONSTRUCTION SCHEDULE

Just as you mark your child's height on a growth chart, the development of their character can be recorded as you build. How do toddlers and preschoolers learn character qualities? The same way they learn to run—first they crawl, then they take baby steps, and finally they take off! Looking back on our efforts at building the characteristics we identified in our first blueprint, there isn't one that has not been vitally important to our children. Some of the qualities have been very easy to shape in one child, and very slow to train in another. Other attributes will come along nicely for a while—then plateau or even regress for a period of time. But aren't adults the same? Complete transformation into Christ's image will take a lifetime.

One Step at a Time

When our lives are Spirit-directed and we allow Him to live His life through us, we will grow in moral excellence, knowledge, self-control, perseverance, godliness, brotherly kindness, and love. These character qualities are said to be the rule, not the exception—and are to be possessed by all Christians—"and are increasing"! (2 Peter 1:3–9 NASB). When we are self-directed (or walking "according to the flesh"), we will spiral downward to become "foolish, disobedient, deceived and enslaved by all kinds of passions and pleasures. We lived in malice and envy, being hated and hating one another" (Titus 3:3 NIV).

The challenge of designing a character plan is overwhelming enough, but the call to be character builders is huge! With that responsibility in mind, you may be trembling right about now! We feel so inadequate because we know our own character flaws are so glaring. How high are God's expectations for our children (and us)? Paul said our goal is to become "complete in Christ" and "filled up to all the fulness of God" (Col. 1:28; Eph. 3:19 NASB).

Expect the Best!

Three bricklayers at work on a job were each asked the same question: "What are you doing?" The first one answered, "Setting a brick." The second said, "Making a wall." The third stated, "I'm building a cathedral."[2] Wouldn't it be awesome if every parent responded to that question with such vision? Imagine a generation full of champions for Christ, shining like stars in a darkened sky. "For you were once darkness, but now you are light in the Lord. Live as children of the light (for the fruit of the light consists in all goodness, righteousness and truth)," (Eph. 5:8–9 NIV). Our fuzzy illusion is growing clearer now. Our pens have ceased from doodling. Our hands take hold of the straightedge of God's Word and we begin. Gentle hands will guide the unsteady apprentice. The great Architect and Engineer is available to perfect and correct us as we help our children build strong permanent lives. Our prayer mirrors Moses' request in Psalm 90:17 (NASB): "And let the favor of the Lord our God be upon us; and do confirm for us the work of our hands; yes, [give permanence to] the work of our hands." Amen to that—now let's begin!

A parent's prayer . . . Father of mercy, I need to confess the countless shortcuts I have attempted in my parenting. You have helped me get very clear on one essential principle—there are none I can afford. Even though I've made too many mistakes to count, You have overcome my weakness to do Your work in the children. It is exciting to look back and see the ways You have built Your qualities in their lives. Right now I need You to keep me on course. Integrity, servanthood, forbearance and other Christlike qualities carry so little weight in our culture today. Yet I know that in Your Kingdom they represent great value. I want our children to grow to become "complete in Christ." I am still a little unclear about Your schedule. I wish I knew when to expect certain behavior and attitudes without my prompting. I will have to depend on You to make it a part of their character. (I guess that's where You have wanted me all along.)

DISCUSSION QUESTIONS

1. What character qualities seem to be in shortest supply among young people today? Why do you think these qualities are missing?

2. What negative impact is the absence of these qualities having on our culture? On your children?

3. Were you raised to be a good citizen or a godly person? How can you distinguish between the two?

4. What is the number one character quality you would like to begin building into your child's life?

8 } Capturing Teachable Moments

"These commandments that I give you today are to be upon your hearts. Impress them on your children."
—Deuteronomy 6:6–7 NIV

Newsweek recently entered the heated debate about how kids develop and asked, "Do Parents Matter?" Judith Rich Harris answered "No," in *The Nurture Assumption: Why Children Turn Out the Way They Do*. She contends that virtually nothing a parent says or does makes a smidgen of difference to what kind of adult the child becomes. What genes don't do, peers do. Her hypothesis stems from her perceptions about her own family of origin and the outcome of parenting her biological and adopted daughters. She was nothing like her parents, and her daughters were poles apart despite the same environments. Her assertions contradict the Bible and the general agreement of a century of child-development research. While she is correct that a child's unique personality is often apparent at birth, and that no two children can be expected to respond in exactly the same way to the same approach, she does a disservice to suggest that it doesn't matter how we treat our children. Her primary recommendation for parents is to move into the best possible neighborhood and surround your child with the peer group that you want them to become like.

After that, it's up to DNA—and your kid's friends—to complete their character development.[1] How does that news grab you?

"Use Your Common Sense!"

Character—whether good or bad—doesn't just happen. From a very early age, children "soak up" character lessons—both positive and negative—that stay with them as adults. Who or what was the greatest character-shaper in your life? If you think back, you may remember specific people or memorable experiences that developed your various attributes. Did your mother spout warnings like "Mabel, Mabel, strong and able, keep your elbows off the table?" As annoying as it was, you haven't forgotten, have you? Until his later years, Solomon was world-renowned for his wisdom. He had prayed for it as a young man. Kings and seekers traveled long distances to consult with him. Solomon spoke more than three thousand proverbs in his lifetime (about eight hundred are found in the book of Proverbs). Their purpose was to give young people the skills and discipline to act with insight, discernment, and discretion. These sayings were taught in riddles, figures, and practical illustrations from daily life, and were passed down from adult to child each generation. Many of your grandparents passed down legacies like the value of hard work, commitment to family, and loyalty to country. Your parents may have exemplified optimism, hospitality, or courage without ever saying a word. Childhood is a series of defining moments influenced by parents, schoolteachers, friends, and leaders who helped you become the person you are today. God has given us the gift of a few critical years to leave a character legacy for our own children.

Make the Most of Teachable Moments

Teachable moments are the framework for character building in everyday situations. They are defined as "neutral" times when children are more open to instruction. Not every character lesson has to be a scheduled, structured time of instruction. In fact, most aren't! The best teachable moments often occur at breakfast, in the car, on walks, in the middle of games, or during bedtime rituals. Integrity can be taught during a tennis game. Discernment can be taught choosing television programs. Diligence can be taught weeding the garden. Courage and perseverance can be taught on a hike. Self-discipline can be taught making beds or buying clothes. Consideration can be taught in a restaurant. The possibilities are endless when we pay attention! God expects us to have His words etched into our own hearts so we won't miss the multitude of character-building opportunities around us. We can take advantage of observations, stories, character studies, word pictures, and object lessons as the events of life unfold. Centuries ago, God revealed the secret of inscribing His commandments on the heart—it's not a list, or a lesson, but a life-style: "Talk about them when you sit at home and when you walk along the road, when you lie down and when you get up. Tie them as symbols on your hands and bind them on your foreheads. Write them on the doorframes of your houses and on your gates" (Deut. 6:7–9 NIV).

Stories, Poems, and Fables

Through the centuries, parents have used all sorts of parables, legends, and family traditions to teach different character qualities. Some of the easiest teachable moments to capture begin before the first birthday, when older infants begin to attend to pictures, rhymes, and finger play. At our house, "Jimmy stories" were born out of constant turmoil over caring for toys. One night I (David) created a simple tale about a boy with a treasured toy that was ruined after he left it outside. The children not only connected with the parable, they began reminding one another about Jimmy! These stories became a ritual and provided an easy vehicle for many other character lessons. Most children look forward to snuggling up to the soothing voice of Mom, Dad, Grandpa, or Auntie— and reading together builds both auditory and visual skills. Classic children's books can spark daily conversations about subjects like friendship, determination, and our favorite theme—cooperation! Bill Bennett compiled hundreds of classical stories into the anthology titled *The Book of Virtues*. Some schools have adopted it as a literature text with units on loyalty, compassion, self-discipline, and friendship.

Our family library maps out the distant road of childhood. *Alice in Wonderland, Pilgrim's Progress, The Hiding Place, Where the Red Fern Grows, Anne of Green Gables*—even *Ramona the Pest*—have taught faithfulness, courage, love, and unselfishness as well as any discourse we have delivered along the way. Even if books did not have a religious theme, we would calligraphy appropriate "character" verses in the end pages. One of the best "series" of teachable moments was reading *The Chronicles of Narnia* by C. S. Lewis together. God used them to ignite the imaginations and sensitive consciences of our youngsters—and they continue to teach vital lessons each time they are reread at different ages.

Observations, Object Lessons, and Word Pictures

Until around age seven, young children are very *concrete* in their learning style, meaning they learn best by seeing, hearing, touching, smelling, and tasting. Abstract learning—the ability to use judgment and reasoning to draw conclusions—develops in later childhood, and is not fully developed until late adolescence. Helping children make observations about firsthand experiences provides a valuable teaching tool for concepts that are difficult to re-create. As a preschooler, Amanda had difficulty maintaining self-control in public places, especially restaurants. One thing that broke the cycle of misbehavior was eating dinner at a table next to a child who was making everyone around him miserable. Quite disgusted, Amanda asked, "Is *that* what *I* act like?" Her observation was the beginning of more pleasant dining experiences for our family!

Elaine often used dolls and puppets to portray characters like

Waldo the Whiner or Casey the Crab, and Big Mouth Frog to indirectly teach a lesson. Watching a puppet react and be corrected provided a nonthreatening way to penetrate their hearts and minds more effectively than Lecture No. 458 ever could! Object lessons use common items to represent abstract ideas—real versus pretend can be demonstrated with the actual fruit and plastic decorations. Word pictures can often describe qualities better than abstract definitions. Anger can be compared to a bumblebee sting, while bitterness is more like a poisonous snakebite. Children can contrast a sharp sting that heals quickly with a piercing bite that makes you very sick for a long time. Older children begin to reason and interpret character lessons from everything they experience. Teenagers begin to assign motives and make judgments about behavior they observe. Character building is an ever-changing process that we hope will evolve into self-instruction over time.

SEEKING THE BEST TEACHABLE MOMENTS

Even though our children are teenagers, we are still trying to capture teachable moments every day. The challenge is greater now than ever, because we are going in so many different directions! One reason early childhood is the best time to start building character is that there is *less competition for attention.* If you haven't set the stage for open communication during the younger years, don't expect it to begin spontaneously during adolescence. Even though we have talked about virtually every subject, our kids have figured out that teachers, coaches—and their peers—often have approaches and agendas they prefer to parental input!

In the Car
Because our school and church are quite a distance from home, we spend a good bit of time in the car every day. We also live an average of twelve hours from both sets of grandparents, so we enjoy plenty of "quality" time on the road each year. A dividend to

all that wear and tear on the cars has been a forum in which to talk and laugh and debate every issue imaginable. Sometimes we read novels together . . . have family meetings—or family fights . . . spiritual discussions . . . private conversations . . . devotionals . . . and prayer time. A teachable tip! There's something magical about those first few minutes after getting in the car. Their conversation is like a dam that opens and lets the water rush out—then stops—causing the water pressure to be less the next time it is opened. Sometimes we rush to be the one to pick up our kids after a practice, or camp, or special activities, because we have come to value the "instant replays" that give so much insight into how their minds and hearts are developing!

During Games

When our children were old enough to play board games, the door opened up for us to teach many new character lessons. One was the value of taking turns, or letting someone else choose the red player. Another was the importance of playing by the rules (mid-game changes are a preschool favorite!). We tried to avoid the words *winner* and *loser* since one of the hardest lessons for adults and children is the art of sportsmanship whether you win or lose. Integrity can also be taught through keeping score. I (David) recall a time when one of the boys and I were playing tennis. I had noticed that he had been struggling with exaggerating in other situations, so I decided to check up on him as we played. In the middle of the game I called out a higher score than what he actually had—and he corrected me with the correct score. That let me know that he was at least *in process* and I could build on that beginning.

Working Together

Ever since we had three in diapers, something always needs cleaning, dusting, vacuuming, or weed-eating. When the children were little, Elaine "tricked" them into thinking that cleaning house was the greatest privilege in the family. She would challenge them with the idea that they were *almost* "big" enough to dust the furniture or Windex the French doors. By the time they figured out what she had done, they were already in the habit of working hard! I have to admit that household tasks and projects have presented unlimited occasions to reinforce character qualities like diligence, servanthood, and teachability. The biggest obstacle to character training during family jobs is the *patience* it takes to teach kids how to perform tasks that would be easier to do yourself. Taking the trouble to instruct smaller steps now will be worth it in the long run, when you have self-motivated, independent young people who have learned the rewards of teamwork at home.

Watching Movies

During the preschool years, we carefully monitored everything our children saw and heard. Part of our character instruction was building discernment. It was apparent that the areas of media and education would be our greatest challenge. There were so many subtle symbols and messages that went against our convictions, so we screened virtually everything the children watched or played with until school age. Once they went to school, we realized that whether they attended public, private, or home schools, we would not always be around to guard their eyes and identify false teachings or point out theory that is taught as fact. One of the most difficult principles to apply to character building is the task of "inoculation." *Inoculate* means to "immunize or protect from disease." A flu shot actually injects a tiny bit of the virus and the body builds up a resistance to it. Likewise, our children need to practice recognizing and evaluating messages that are opposed to what God says in Scripture. "But solid food is for the mature, who by constant use have trained themselves to distinguish good from evil" (Heb. 5:14 NIV). During elementary school we began to devise ways to help our children "practice" discernment. We allowed the kids to apply the "eight-point rating system" to determine whether their minds should dwell on music or programs we knew were "borderline." Using Philippians 4:8, they judged: Is it true? Noble? Right? Pure? Lovely? Admirable? Excellent? Praiseworthy? If they didn't add up, we placed them in the "worthless" category. We found out that much of the adult entertainment we excused didn't measure up either. It is comforting to observe young teens who recognize error mixed with truth in a textbook, or discard a CD with lyrics that "stink." We encourage you to develop their "radar system" so your children will be ready when the world comes knocking at your door.

Mealtimes

Call us the Cleavers, but we are one of the endangered species who have hung on to the tradition of regular family dinners. Elaine doesn't wear pearls, and we don't eat in the dining room much, but several nights a week we eat dinner together—at the table. Dinner is family time—and everyone participates. Mealtimes are the training ground for many character lessons involving respect. They are the best venue for practicing public manners—with the reward of dinner out for those who display them! We have used mealtime for family devotions, group discussions, and character studies, with mixed results. One fall we chose a character quality each week as our focus. We would introduce it early in the week and discuss it each night during dinner. The children were commissioned to look for examples of that quality (or the absence of it) during each day. Centering "table-talks" around holidays, like Advent and Easter, has also opened the doors for teachable moments. Other formats haven't been so successful! At every stage, limited time or short attention spans place certain limits on overstructuring after a meal. For us, the most effective, more "formal" teachable moments have been before an early bedtime.

The Bedtime Ritual

When our children reached adolescence, they finally realized that naptime and bedtime are not a curse of childhood. They love to sleep whenever they can! However, at eight months of age, they suddenly realized that they might be missing something fun by going to sleep before we did. That was when we initiated our first bedtime "ritual." It included snuggling up, reading a story, praying, and singing a bedtime song before the lights went out and the door was closed. As time went on, the ritual continued, but the content of our conversations and prayers began to expand. Bedtime was a family forum, with everyone piled on one bed. Other times were reserved for private discussions or instruction. Issues that were never brought up in the daytime always seemed to filter to the surface as they relaxed. After fifteen years, we still hear adult-size voices call us to their bedsides—though our ritual rarely includes reading or singing anymore. But the teachable moments are still there—even within the most sophisticated teenager's "sanctuary." In their own time they will tell the best and the worst of their day. They listen when we mention qualities they thought we hadn't noticed. And they still want to hear that they are your "favorite" (even though they know you'll tell the others the same thing!).

Redeeming the Unexpected

Parents eventually learn to *expect* the unexpected. When Blake and Joel were eight years old, I (David) began to wonder aloud to Elaine about the right time for discussing sexuality with the boys—it's part of character building, too! We had worked so hard to guard their eyes and maintain their innocence, and I definitely wanted to be the first to initiate that conversation. Since there were no real signs of interest at that point, we put it on the back burner for a while. Several weeks later, when I was traveling, Elaine called with the news that our boys had been exposed to illegal, hard-core pornography. My heart sank as she described how their buddies found magazines in a drainpipe with perversions that our eyes could barely interpret. Abruptly, I canceled the remainder of my trip. I drove all night to get home and address the confusion and nausea they felt every time they remembered what they saw. Looking back, that horrible experience opened the door—not just for "the talk"—but for the beginning of an ongoing conversation that has continued into the teenage years. Amanda had a more gentle introduction to the subject of sexuality, thanks to a wonderful book called *How and When to Tell Your Kids About Sex.*[2] Now we are thankful to enjoy the freedom to openly support our children through the years where purity and perversion are bound to collide!

WILL MY WORK EVER BE FINISHED?

The Taj Mahal is one of the world's most beautiful buildings. It was built in the 1600s by the ruler of India as a memorial to his wife. There is some uncertainty about who really drew the plans— some believe it was a pupil of the greatest Turkish architect of his time. The whole building is covered in pure white marble. More than twenty-two thousand workers labored daily for twenty-two years to complete the huge edifice, which stands on a square marble base. Apart from geometrical designs, most of the building is covered in verses from the Koran, which are calligraphied into the marble.[3]

God wants to shape your child into one of this generation's greatest wonders. In the next two decades, your work will be completed. The goal is a splendid memorial to the One who is our Life. Remember who has been overseeing your design. If you'll refer to your blueprint regularly, you will stay on track more consistently. The strength of your foundation is critical. Do not despair when it seems that you'll never live to see the end product of all your labor. Don't expect godly character to spring forth after a few months.

Grand edifices require years to complete! You'll see the framework after the first few years. The wiring will be installed as habits become more ingrained. God's Word should be evident in the finished design. And the light from inside will emanate to everyone who comes near. It will be worth everything if you will continue in partnership with the Author and Finisher of our faith.

A parent's prayer . . . All this talk about the lack of influence parents have on their children makes me mad, Lord. Why are we always debating things You established long ago? The family was the very first institution You set up. Why aren't people listening? Why don't I listen more to you and less to my peers? You have placed three children in my classroom. Help me to make the most of this time, because very soon they will be graduating. Don't let me get stale or too predictable—or too impatient—as their primary teacher. Give me Your creativity and energy to capture the teachable moments You have scheduled. Etch Your lessons on my heart first, so I'll be ready to pour them into my children when those moments present themselves.

DISCUSSION QUESTIONS

1. How can you know whether the family or the environment is having more influence on your child's life?

2. Where and when have you had the most success capturing teachable moments? The least?

3. What area of capturing teachable moments can you add to your life-style of character training right away?

4. Until now, has your character training reflected that a godly person develops by accident or by design? How will you be more purposeful during the next six months?

Part Three:

Training Your Child

———On October 29, 1998, John Glenn was among seven astronauts aboard the space shuttle Discovery. Although shuttle missions have become almost "ho-hum" the last several years, this one sparked great interest because Glenn was seventy-seven years old at the time of the launch! Thirty-six years earlier, John Glenn was the first American to orbit the earth in space. Glenn's adventurous courage, superior training, and lifelong dreams prepared him for another "first." Now he has become the oldest astronaut to take part in the exploration of new possibilities benefiting future generations.

The requirements for the first pilot astronauts were that they be less than forty years old, and in excellent physical condition. In addition, they had to have a degree in engineering, at least 1,500 hours of flying time, and have graduated from a test-pilot school as a qualified jet pilot. Initially, there were five hundred volunteers, but selection criteria were increased as the demands and expertise evolved. Selected applicants received demanding instruction to gain familiarity with three-dimensional motion, weightlessness, and other special characteristics of space travel. Special simulators helped trainees practice and perfect their specific functions. Eventually, the scientist-astronaut was added who, in addition to physical and psychological excellence, was required to have a Ph.D. in medicine, engineering, or science. All astronauts were to receive additional training in meteorology, guidance and navigation, astronomy, physics, and computer science. They had to maintain excellent physical condition and flight readiness at all times—yet only handfuls were selected to participate in each mission.

Parents have the opportunity to prepare their children for the exciting and challenging "missions" that God is already planning for the next generation. The requirements will be great, so the criteria must be set high. Trainees must have appropriate instruction for the world in which they must navigate. They will need continuous opportunities to practice their responsibilities in the safety of a "simulator." Many parents have great dreams about the future, but how many children will really be ready to launch out into our changing culture? Parents who aim high and train their children diligently are following American legends, like John Glenn, toward discovering what now seems impossible and unimaginable! The countdown has already started, so let's take off into the next four chapters and develop your training program according to God's design.

9 } Untangling Discipline's Definition

"Train up a child in the way he should go,
And when he is old he will not depart from it."
—Proverbs 22:6 *NKJV*

Despite all the books written on discipline, most parents still struggle to respond correctly when a child spills his milk, reprograms the computer, or bites the neighbor's child. That reminds me of a little girl who was walking along sobbing noisily, when a kind gentleman asked her what the trouble was. She said (between sniffles), "My mother lost her psychology book and now she's using her own judgment!"[1] The good news is that parents don't need a psychology degree for discipline, because we already possess the most reliable source on the subject—the Bible.

THE TWO SIDES OF DISCIPLINE

The majority limit the term *discipline* to mean "punishment," when it represents so much more. Discipline is actually a two-sided coin with instruction on one side and correction on the other. If you want to partake from a linguistic spaghetti bowl, try a word study on *discipline!* Words like *teaching, instruction, training, reproof, rebuke, chastening, chastisement* (and *punish-*

ment) crisscross throughout the various Bible translations. The New American Standard Bible (NASB) might use *discipline* to mean "instruction," while the New International Version (NIV) uses it to mean "correction." In the King James Version (KJV), *discipline* is only used one time in the entire Bible! Comparing the Hebrew and Greek words helps us sort out some of the different meanings:

> *Instruction*—tutoring, education, nurture, training
> *Correction*—reforming, rectifying, restoring, and improving character
> *Reproof*—conviction, evidence, testing, discovery
> *Rebuke*—dispute, reason, convince, or justify
> *Punishment*—inflict a penalty or fine—even condemn
> *Chastening*—with blows or words to warn, restrain, or check.[2]

ONE WORD: *TRAINING*

If you had to pick one word that best defines *discipline,* it would be *training.* If you had to choose one verse that best sums up training, it would be Proverbs 22:6. This familiar verse is to parenting what John 3:16 is to evangelism. When used as an action verb, *train* describes breaking a wild horse and bringing it into submission by using a rope in the mouth. The original Hebrew word for "train" is the term used for the palate, the roof of the mouth, or the gums. It is also used to describe developing a thirst, as a midwife massaged the gums of a newborn with date juice to help a baby begin nursing. Proper training should actually develop *a thirst to obey.* Imagine that! Young people often cite athletic coaches, youth directors, and music teachers as important influences of their character. Perhaps it is because they not only teach skills but go an extra step. Training challenges a person to apply and practice the knowledge he has been taught. Teaching deals with the *intellect (I know what is right)* while training deals with the *will (I choose what is right)*. Former Dallas Cowboys coach Tom Landry summed it up well: "I have a job to do that isn't that complicated but is often very difficult—to get a group of men to do what they *don't want to do* so they can achieve what they've wanted to do all of their lives."[3]

DISCIPLINE SHAPES LIVES

A hammer is a very powerful tool. If used violently or carelessly, you could use it to destroy something. On the other hand, when placed in the hands of a skillful craftsman, a hammer can be a very beneficial tool for crafting something handsome. Discipline is like a hammer. It can be used constructively as a tool—or destructively as a weapon. You probably need protection when your curious toddler is upsetting your pantry or your boisterous teens are wrestling near your prized lamp! Discipline is meant to be used as a tool to creatively train and mold the self-control that may prevent such episodes. Ultimately, discipline—or training—will be the vehicle for molding the character qualities you drafted into your blueprint. When you think of a child, you probably picture someone under twelve, but throughout the Old Testament, *child* is a broad term covering all the years under a parent's care. However, don't wait until they are about to leave home to begin, since discipline can have long-term—even eternal—effects.

DISCIPLINE DEMONSTRATES LOVE

Some people say, "I love my children too much to discipline them." Unwittingly, those parents have been deceived. They must view "discipline" only as punishment—surely they don't mean they love their children too much to *instruct* them. Hebrews 12:6 (NIV) says, "The Lord disciplines those he loves, and he punishes everyone he accepts as a son." Eli was one father who made a fatal mistake in this area. He was in full-time ministry and apparently spent more time scrutinizing other people's behavior than watching what his two sons were up to. They were described as "worthless men" (NASB) and "corrupt; they did not know the LORD" (1 Sam. 2:12 NKJV). While Eli was perched outside the temple, they were inside cheating others and perverting worship. Eli was the last to know, but even then he didn't take action to correct them. God identified Eli's sin: "You . . . honor your sons more than Me" (1 Sam. 2:29 NKJV). And "his sons made themselves vile, and he did not restrain them" (1 Sam. 3:13 NKJV). Even after God's prophetic warning, nothing changed, so God took matters into His own hands. Eventually, both sons were killed while guarding the symbolic ark of the covenant. When Eli heard the news, he fell over dead (literally). In the end, the rebellion of two sons (and their passive father) had affected their community—and the nation of Israel—since their emblem of God's protection and blessing was stolen when they died. Are we overdramatic to suggest that *America* could be affected if parents do not discipline their children? Considering the permissive upbringing of the generation currently leading our country— and in light of the mass of confused young people today—maybe the stretch isn't all that far.

DISCIPLINE DRAWS HEARTS

Peter challenged parents to personally receive and identify with the gospel, then extended the promise to future generations: "For the promise is to you and to your children, and to all who are afar off, as many as the Lord our God will call" (Acts 2:39 NKJV). God uses Christian parents to draw their children to Himself. As you train them to distinguish right from wrong, they are preparing to grasp the concepts of righteousness and sin. Our aim is that the pattern of obedience to earthly parents will ultimately lead to a pattern of obedience to the heavenly Father.

DISCIPLINE REQUIRES OBEDIENT PARENTS

Obedience means acting on the commands and decisions of another. The object of discipline is to form a pattern of obedience. This may be harder for some than others. Although I (Elaine) was an agreeable child for the most part, I had a bad habit of "sassing" my parents. They said, "You'd argue with a bull in a china cabinet!" but never broke that habit. Sometimes I still struggle with that trait as an adult—and one of our children has "inherited" that lovely tendency. Because neither of us has finished our training process, we often go several rounds in the proverbial china cabinet! God must get frustrated at having to simultaneously train the student *and* the teacher. Despite our own failings, we need a high standard for compliance. In Genesis 22:1–14, Abraham modeled the kind of obedience we desire for our children. Like most people, he learned to obey God the hard way! Once he did learn, he was able to transfer that same pattern of obedience to his son. When God told Abraham to sacrifice Isaac (whose birth in itself was a miracle), he obeyed without delay. Even this bizarre mandate didn't cause Abraham to complain or argue. He believed God's promises were trustworthy and had matured enough to accept that God knows what He is doing even when we don't. When God gave specific instructions, Abraham carried them out to the letter. He knew from experience that God's plan is the best (and only) way. Do you obey God *immediately, respectfully, and completely?* If not, is it fair to expect that from your child?

The obedience transferred to Isaac surpasses Abraham's example of submission. After all, Isaac was about to be sacrificed on a burning altar! Genesis 22:6–9 reveals that Isaac demonstrated the same characteristics as his father. Scholars say he was probably old enough to physically resist his aging father, yet he meekly allowed himself to be bound. His only question was, "Where is the lamb for the burnt offering?" When Abraham assured him that God would provide it, he obeyed without objection. Both of them had total confidence in a living God who could even resurrect the dead. Ultimately, God honored the *immediate, respectful, complete* obedience of the father and son. Few of your children's peers will be required to obey according to this standard, but it is a worthy aim to pursue. We are not suggesting a militant approach of molding silent soldiers, but learning to obey *quickly* may save your child's life someday. *Respectful* submission will reinforce positive attitudes that will help them get along with authority figures they encounter. Finally, *complete* obedience helps prevent future regrets and painful consequences.

Discipline Avoids Regrets

James Dobson stated that "discipline is like baking a cake—you don't realize you have a disaster until it is too late!"[4] This news is both exciting and terrifying to those who believe there is plenty of time to train for the future. The last phrase in Proverbs 22:6 (NIV) says, "And when he is old he will not turn from it." There are some parents who were attentive to discipline, but their children made ungodly choices anyway. Perhaps this verse is meant to encourage them that their rebellious child will return to the Lord by the time they are elderly. Interestingly, the word *old* means "hair on the chin" as well as "bearded one." Why do we assume that all teenagers will reject their early training in adolescence? If you have trained diligently from infancy, you might see maturity by the "peach fuzz" years. It will be worth it to pursue excellence in our training so that regardless of the choices they make in the future, we won't have the burden of knowing we didn't give it our best.

Discipline Must Be Personalized

Because our kids are close in age, we have observed how differently three people can respond within a similar environment.

Blake and Joel are identical twins—one half of the same egg, sharing all the same genes and chromosomes—yet from day one they have been as individually wired as any two human beings. Each of them has displayed characteristics of their birth order even though they are only nine minutes apart. Blake has been everyone's image of a firstborn. Joel is the stereotypical middle child. Amanda is definitely the baby—and the princess, being the only girl. All three have unique dispositions and patterns that emerged early and have remained basically the same over time. Proverbs 22:6 says "Train a child in the way he should go . . ." The word *in* means "in keeping with," or literally, the way he is *bent*. God has created every child with unique traits causing them to "give" more easily in one direction than another. Some children cry if you look at them "sideways." A reminder motivates others, and others only respond after a threat. If you have more than one child, you know that what works with one may have no effect on the other. This does not mean that children should not be trained *in God's way*. It does mean you will find less resistance when you apply an individualized strategy for each personality type.

DISCIPLINE MUST BEGIN EARLY

Before our children went to kindergarten, they could recite, "Children, obey your parents in all things, for this is well pleasing to the Lord" (Col. 3:20 NKJV). We hoped it would "rub off" when they became teenagers! Parents have a tendency to worry ahead of time about "big" things like drugs, pregnancy, and gangs to the exclusion of "smaller" things like manners, hard work, and respectful responses. Luke 16:10 provides an important principle for developing obedience in everything—start with little things! "Anyone who can be trusted in little matters can also be trusted in important matters. But anyone who is dishonest in little matters will be dishonest in important matters" (CEV). If we hope to see the day when our kids will come home from their dates on time or resist cheating even when "everyone else is doing it," we must establish obedience in related areas when they are young. Respect for teachers and other authority figures starts with the toddler being taught to say yes (instead of *uh-huh*), please, and thank you, and other expressions of esteem and appreciation for others. Responsibility for cars, stereos, and furniture begins with preschoolers who first learn to care for Big Wheels, tape players, and dollhouses.

A Fish Story

He was eleven years old, and went fishing every chance he got from the dock at his family's cabin on an island in the middle of a New Hampshire lake. On the day before the bass season opened, he and his father were fishing in the evening, catching sunfish and perch with worms. When his pole doubled over, he knew something was on the other end. His father watched with admiration as the boy skillfully worked the fish alongside the dock. Finally he very gingerly lifted the exhausted fish from the water. It was the largest one he had ever seen, but it was a bass. The father lit a match and looked at his watch. It was 10:00 P.M.—two hours before the season opened. He looked at the fish, then at the boy. "You'll have to put it back, son," he said. "Dad!" cried the boy. "There will be other fish," said his father. "Not as big as this one," cried the boy. Even though no one had seen them, nor could anyone ever know what time he caught the fish, the boy could tell by the clarity of his father's voice that the decision was not negotiable. He slowly worked the hook out of the lip of the huge bass, and lowered it into the black water. The boy suspected that he would never again see such a great fish. Thirty-four years later, the boy is a successful architect in New York City. His father's cabin is still there on the island in the middle of the lake. He takes his own son and daughters fishing from the same dock. And he was right. He has never again caught such a magnificent fish as the one he landed that night long ago. But he does see the same fish—again and again—every time he comes up against a question of ethics. Do *we* do right when no one is looking? Do we refuse to cut corners to get the design in on time? Or refuse to trade stocks based on information that we know we aren't supposed to have? We would if we were taught to put the fish back when we were young.[5]

DISCIPLINE REAPS REWARDS

A man found a cocoon containing an emperor moth, and took it home to watch the rare butterfly emerge. One day a small opening appeared, and for several hours the moth struggled but couldn't seem to force its body past a certain point. Deciding something was wrong, the man took scissors and snipped the remaining bit of cocoon. The moth emerged easily, its body large and swollen, the wings small and shriveled. He expected that in a few hours the wings would spread out in their natural beauty, but they did not. Instead of developing into a creature free to fly, the moth spent its life dragging around a swollen body and shriveled wings. The constricting cocoon and the struggle necessary to pass through the tiny opening are the Creator's way of forcing fluid from the body into the wings. The "merciful" snip was, in reality, cruel.[6]

> No discipline seems pleasant at the time, but painful. Later on, however, it produces a harvest of righteousness and peace for those who have been trained by it. Therefore, strengthen your feeble arms and weak knees. Make level paths for your feet, so that the lame may not be disabled, but rather healed. (Heb. 12:11–12 NIV).

Instructing and correcting your children will present struggles for them—and for you. Don't be afraid that a high standard for behavior will hinder your child in the future. Someday you'll see that your labor and their training did not "cripple" them, but actually released them to "fly."

DISCIPLINE IS AN ADVENTURE!

Remember that first tiny trike propelled by fat little feet? All too soon comes the Big Wheel, then the two-wheeler—with training wheels, of course. One of the great passages of childhood is the day when your child rides alone for the first time—wobbling a little or heading for a lamppost—but all by themselves! Parents are like a set of training wheels. They steady the rider until he can take over the handlebars and pedal on his own. Preferably, there is one parent on each side of the child. (Single parents may need a family member or friend for added balance.) Both training wheels need to touch the ground to keep the rider upright. Parents who are "on the same page" regarding their goals for discipline, will be able to keep their child from falling as easily. The tough thing about training wheels is that eventually they are meant to be removed. You would think something was wrong if a teenager was still using training wheels. Parents are called to come alongside their children and provide intensive training during the childhood years. Soon enough you will find yourself standing in the middle of the street, watching your child ride beyond your view. But for now, screw those training wheels on tight and get ready for the ride of your lives!

A parent's prayer . . . *Thank You, Holy Spirit, for being our Teacher, and correcting my mindset about discipline. Help it sink in that my goal is training—not just restraining. You know how much I love the children, yet I constantly point out their weaknesses and errors more than the things they are doing right. Help me develop "radar" that searches out positive actions and attitudes that I can affirm. (Particularly the child who I am now thinking of.) I haven't balanced instruction and correction, and I need you to make up for any*

*lost time. Give me the resolve to complete my task in a way that will
leave little room for regrets in the future. Do you have any regrets
with me?*

DISCUSSION QUESTIONS

1. Why is discipline such a controversial subject today?

2. How balanced has your discipline been between instruction and correction? Try to explain why.

3. How could you respond to the parent who says, "I love my child too much to punish him"?

4. Whose example has had the largest impact on your current parenting style?

5. Which of these discipline principles impacted you the most?

   a. Discipline means training.
   b. Discipline shapes lives.
   c. Discipline demonstrates love.
   d. Discipline draws hearts.
   e. Discipline requires obedient parents.

Devising a Winning Strategy

"Train yourself to be godly."
—*1 Timothy 4:7* NIV

Dear Ann Landers: I'm a 16-year-old girl who is a nervous wreck from getting yelled at. All I hear from morning till night is, "Stop smoking, get off the phone, hang up your clothes, do your homework, and clean up your room." How can I get them off my case?

Sick of Parents

Dear Sick: Stop smoking, get off the phone, hang up your clothes, do your homework, and clean up your room.[1]

If only it were that simple. If you have children over three years old, chances are you have plenty of games in your home. Our first board games included classics like Candyland, Hi-Ho Cherry-O, and Chutes and Ladders. Before long, our children graduated to "junior" games—Jr. Pictionary, Jr. Monopoly, Jr. Clue—but they wanted to play *real* Monopoly and *real* Clue! Finally, they began to pick up games that required more problem solving like Checkers and Spades. Discipline is like a game—but not like Candyland or Junior games or even Checkers. The Discipline Game requires real skill and tactics—like Backgammon or Chess. Just as we need a blueprint for character building, we need a well thought-out strategy for discipline. The good news is that if you learn to play the Discipline Game, well, everyone wins!

ORGANIZING YOUR BEHAVIOR GOALS

Actions lead to habits. Habits lead to character. Character defines identity. If that is true, the discipline process will follow an orderly progression from birth to twelve years of age. If your children have missed the "ideal" age for training, do not give up! Begin wherever they are and apply the same steps outlined below. You will be encouraged to know that God can overrule everything— and there is nothing that can't be redeemed!

Action

Ideally, the first "training block" should be introduced between birth to five. As children are trained to *do right*, they gradually learn which actions and attitudes are appropriate in various situations. Little children will need lots of repetition and specific explanations before they can remember what you want them to do. The key word for this training block is *Practice*!

Habit

The second training block can be added during the elementary years—between approximately six and twelve years of age. If they have been trained to *do right* during the preschool years, they should be ready to learn to *do right consistently*. The goal of this phase is to reinforce proper actions and attitudes until they become habits. This is also a good time to explain the logical and biblical reasons for your guidelines and boundaries. The key word for this training block is *Reinforce*!

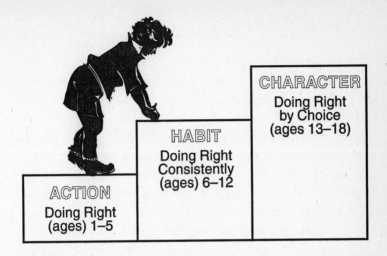

ACTION
Doing Right
(ages) 1–5

HABIT
Doing Right
Consistently
(ages) 6–12

CHARACTER
Doing Right
by Choice
(ages 13–18)

Character

During the third training block—the teenage years—youth who have learned to *do right consistently* can be evaluated to learn if they will *do right by choice*. Once your children reach middle school, the results of your early training should begin to spring forth. This is the age when parents hope that *good* character will emerge. The key word for this training block is *Pray!*

CHOOSING AGE-APPROPRIATE BEHAVIOR GOALS

Even a child is known by his actions, by whether his conduct
is pure and right. (Prov. 20:11 NIV)

Did you know that training can begin even in infancy? During the first seven months, your primary goal may be for your baby to adapt to a regular schedule and to sleep through the night. Creepers and crawlers need training, too—mainly about safe ways to explore their expanding world. From twelve to twenty-four months, rapid language development allows your training to become more direct.

Ask, "What am I trying to train?"

This is one of the most important questions a parent should ask throughout parenthood. Your character blueprint contains the big picture. Your behavior goals will represent the "baby steps" for reaching your goals. Regardless of your child's age, most of your goals can be sorted into two categories.

Respect. Preference, esteem, admiration, honor. God thought it was important enough to "sandwich" it right in the middle of the Ten Commandments. The first four commandments address our relationship to God. The last five commandments deal with our relationship to people. Exodus 20:12 states, "Honor your father and your mother, that your days may be long upon the land which the LORD your God is giving you" (NKJV). Respect for parents precedes honor for God or other people. Toddlers begin by learning to respond to commands like "Come here," "No-no," and "Stop." Even two-year-olds can understand "Make your eyes look at me" and "Obey quickly." Why not teach early talkers to answer "yes" (rather than "yeah")? As older preschoolers, they can easily add "Yes, sir" and "No, ma'am." Other training goals include the proper way to interrupt a conversation, ask a question, and register a protest calmly. School-age children can learn how to use the telephone correctly, to shake hands with adults, to maintain eye contact in conversations, and to practice the manners of a young lady or gentleman at home and in public.

Responsibility. Reliability, accountability, trustworthiness for yourself (then others). When your children grow up, they will be accountable for their own actions the same way you are. Training them in this area of discipline is essential for becoming independent later. Use these goals to allow toddlers to feel "big" during their struggle for power and autonomy. They can learn so many things that will begin to free you up. They can be trained to feed themselves, bring you objects, and help sponge spills and pick up toys. Preschoolers can begin to help with family jobs, dress themselves, take care of their toys, and clean up their "creative" messes.

School-age children will require instruction about keeping up with homework, learning to manage their time and money, as well as making wise choices about clothes and friends.

Consider Action and Attitude

Some parents set rules and guidelines for outward behavior without considering the demeanor with which their child obeys. Remember that our ideal for obedience was to respond (1) immediately, (2) respectfully, and (3) completely. That means more than the physical act of carrying out your direct command. By the age of three or four—if not before—the attitude component of obedience has already presented itself. You may have heard about the child who had been sent to the corner. She was sitting on a little chair when she whispered to her doll, "I'm sitting down on the outside, but I'm standing up on the inside!" We have had a lot of experience with this at our house! Signs of *disobedience in attitude* include a sour face, "poochy" lips, grumbling, sassing, arguing, negotiating, sulking, eye-rolling, and true tantrums. Any one of them is a "red flag" signaling you to emphasize the category of respect.

SETTING GUIDELINES AND BOUNDARIES TOGETHER

Two are better than one because they have a good return for their labor. For if either of them falls, the one will lift up his companion. But woe to the one who falls when there is not another to lift him up. (Eccl. 4:9–10 NASB)

Behavior goals should include a balance between guidelines and boundaries. Guidelines are the actions and attitudes you want to *occur*. Boundaries are the actions and attitudes you want to *avoid*. The chances are pretty good that you and your spouse were disciplined differently during childhood. If your parents were too permissive, you may lean toward a stricter approach with your kids. If your spouse's parents were too authoritarian, he may resist putting any restrictions on your children. One of the worst things that can happen to a couple is to send mixed signals about what is appropriate or inappropriate—it will definitely come back to haunt you! Disagreements about discipline are not uncommon, but disharmony will give your child the upper hand to play you against one another. As difficult as it may be, couples should determine to agree on one set of "family rules." You will become more confident trainers when you function as a team with the same game plan.

A Word of Grace

Let us insert a word of encouragement (and caution) to unmarried parents, divorced parents, and stepparents. One of your biggest challenges may be a former spouse who seems to be undoing everything you are trying to build. Lynda Hunter wrote a practical guide from a Christian perspective called *Parenting on Your Own*. She emphasized the importance of cooperation between both parents for the sake of the children—regardless of your feelings about each other.[2] The only way to make this happen is for each parent to focus on the interests and needs of the *children* and pinpoint win-win solutions for *them*. Unfortunately, you can't control the behavior of the other parent. This is where married couples simply must draw single moms and dads into their circle of friends for support and encouragement. Whether married or single, parents need to get together in groups from time to time, to brainstorm, counsel, and pray together. Don't forget the many millions of grandparents raising families for the second time—please include them as well.

In *Grandparenting by Grace,* Irene Endicott pointed out that the adjustments and sacrifices required of grandparents elicit strong emotions ranging from anger and grief to guilt or self-pity. They need financial advisers, parenting classes, community support—and possibly a competent attorney.[3] God reserves special blessings for every person who is in a less than ideal parenting situation. You can help your children break the cycle of unhealthy patterns from the past. Don't let any person or circumstance rob you of that hope!

PREDETERMINING GUIDELINES AND BOUNDARIES

Without consultation, plans are frustrated,
But with many counselors they succeed. (Prov. 15:22 NASB)

Although you will never be able to think of every situation that will arise, you can identify quite a few that are common to all children. If you have not anticipated the universal situations that are bound to come up, you may be caught off guard and react in a way that you and the child will pay for later! Someone will flush, eat, or spill something horrible at some point and we will overreact. Setting realistic, practical guidelines takes some ingenuity. (See Appendix C for age-appropriate behavior goals.) One of your behavior goals may be *responsible table manners*. Experience dictates that children will occasionally spill at the table; however, some preplanned table rules may protect your suit from a glass of milk before that major presentation at the office. Your guidelines may include: "Use a lid on the cup." "Hold the cup with both hands." "Keep the cup on the place mat." When your family rules are determined ahead of time, you are better able to respond to an accidental spill when it happens. Of course, there will always be unpredictable disasters like the one our former baby-sitter encountered. When our boys were ten, Stephanie kept them on the days Elaine worked at the hospital. At the beginning of the summer, we gave her a list of family rules so she would be prepared. She worried that so many rules would make them dislike her—so she ignored them! One day, the boys locked her inside the swimming pool gate for a couple of hours until a neighbor rescued her. Elaine made them lie down until she could get in touch with David and figure out how on earth to respond to *that one!* That was just one of many situations we have had to team up on!

Recording Your Strategy

Let's walk through another example, using the reproducible Behavior Goal Worksheets (see Appendices B-1 and B-2). After consulting your character blueprint, one of your character goals may be *self-control.* Self-control is primarily an issue of respect. An age-appropriate behavior goal for a six-year-old would be to demonstrate *good sportsmanship* during games—specifically, winning and losing graciously. Once a behavior goal is identified, you must establish your family's *guidelines* and *boundaries* regarding sportsmanship. Your family rule might be to congratulate your opponent when you lose and to encourage your opponent when you win. Your boundaries might be not to cry or pout over a loss and not to gloat or "trash-talk" over a victory.

> What am I trying to train? (Consult character blueprint)
> Character Quality: *Self-control*
> Category: *Respect*
> Training Ground: *Competitive games*
> Behavior Goal: *Good sportsmanship during games.*
> Guidelines: *Congratulate the winner. Encourage the loser.*
> Boundaries: *Keep your temper. Do not brag.*

COMMUNICATING GUIDELINES AND BOUNDARIES CLEARLY

> Be prepared in season and out of season; correct, rebuke and encourage—with great patience and careful instruction.
> (2 Tim. 4:2 NIV).

In *Point Man,* Steve Farrar shared a story told by David Roper. His family was at a conference center and he and his wife were seated with the conference director in the lodge. Right behind the lodge was a recently seeded embankment with signs that said, *KEEP OFF THE BANK*. Suddenly, the conference director jumped up and shouted, "Stay off the bank!" and ran out the door. To Roper's horror, there was one of his boys poised right at the top of the bank. Mortified, Roper took him around the building, got a little switch, and kept saying, "Son, didn't you hear that man say 'Stay off the bank'?" As they walked back, the little boy looked up with tearstained eyes and asked, "Daddy, what's a bank?"[4]

Become Fluent in "Childrenese"

Parents may establish rules easily enough, but they must be communicated meaningfully on the child's language level before expecting obedience. The secret is patience and persistence. We must make it simple enough for two-year-olds with basic statements like "Make your feet stop" or "Toys go in the basket." Once we figure out how to translate our wishes we must repeat them many times to establish understanding. You will have to test and retest, explaining new concepts, then saying, "Make your eyes look at me" (toddlers); or asking, "What did Daddy say?" (preschoolers); or, "What is our rule about . . . ?" (older children) until it gets settled in their minds. Later you will begin to discern disobedience from honest confusion or feigned ignorance!

Explain the Purposes Behind Family Rules

This is love, that we walk according to His commandments. This is the commandment, that as you have heard from the beginning, you should walk in it. (2 John 6 NKJV)

Even though very young children may not pick up on all the meaning, it is never too soon to explain why you set different guidelines and boundaries. When you tell your child to stay on the driveway, you can add, "This is our rule because we want you to stay safe." Kids resent the attitude of "Just because I said so." It does not inspire obedience or help build character. However, there are times when it will be appropriate to say, "God has made me responsible for you and I have a bad feeling about your doing that." Children who recognize that your motivation is love and concern are more ready to comply with your wishes. Remember the developmental stages of action, habit, and character? The habit stage (ages six to twelve) is a critical period for passing on the logical and biblical principles that will help them choose to do right on their own. Sharing Scripture to back up discipline also confirms that your aims are also God's will.

DISTINGUISHING THE CHILD'S INTENT

There have been too many horrifying news stories about parents who harmed or even killed infants who wouldn't stop crying or toddlers who broke something valuable. Parents of young children must ask themselves a vital question before responding to negative behavior or disobedience. Was it childish irresponsibility or willful disobedience? How you respond to ignorance or immaturity is different from your response to deliberate noncompliance. The aim is to adjust your consequences to the child's intent.

Ignorance: A seven-month-old exploring a plug is unaware of its danger. A two-year-old touching a lightbulb is uneducated about burned fingers. A four-year-old who puts the car into gear doesn't know that it will roll down the hill. These children need supervision, redirection, and instruction.

Immaturity: A fifteen-month-old pulling a full pitcher out of the refrigerator is impulsive. A two-year-old making waves overflow from the tub is careless. A six-year-old playing with a slingshot is reckless. An eight-year-old losing a library book is irresponsible. In most cases, these children need instruction and logical consequences (see Chapter Eleven).

Defiance: The parent must identify and extinguish the earliest sparks of rebellion—whether it comes out as a challenge, a dare, or a full-fledged revolt! New parents will quickly learn to recognize the gleam in the eye that distinguishes between these three responses. Usually between eight and eighteen months, a parent can identify the expression that communicates, "I know exactly what you're saying and I'm going to do it my way!" These children will need a combination of the discipline tools Chapter Eleven will describe.

RESPONDING TO BOTH OBEDIENCE AND DISOBEDIENCE

"Do not be deceived, God is not mocked; for whatever a man sows, that he will also reap." Galatians 6:7–9 (NKJV) contains a law of sowing that can't be overridden—when you plant seeds, they produce a harvest. If you don't plant, you don't reap. If you plant pumpkins, you won't get watermelons. The harvest is the evidence of what was planted. This illustration is often used to warn about bad behavior, but sometimes we forget that the sowing principle works both ways. "And let us not grow weary while doing good, for in due season we shall reap if we do not lose heart" (Gal. 6:9 NKJV). What a promise for parents to hold on to.

The Role of Consequences
There should always be a consequence whether the child responds in disobedience or obedience. Consequences teach the child that every action and attitude matters to you and to God. If there is no consequence after disobedience, children eventually learn that sin has no price. Likewise, if there is no consequence for obedience, children eventually become discouraged about the futility of trying to please you—or God. Parents often wait to respond until a child disobeys. Try to catch the good behavior, then respond so they don't "lose heart" and "grow weary" of doing right. Many times the harvest they hope to reap is your attention and if sowing disobedience gets the job done, a large crop of disobedience will be harvested! When we are careful to notice and

praise our child's proper actions, words, and attitudes, they will become more motivated to sow seeds of goodness and kindness. During the first week of sixth grade, the boys were getting used to having male teachers for the first time. On the first day, the science teacher told the class to be sitting quietly with their books ready when he walked into the room. The next day, he came into class and asked anyone who had been talking before he arrived to join him in the hall. Joel was one of several who came forward for punishment. When they got outside, the teacher handed each one a Gold Homework Pass and congratulated them for showing so much integrity. Joel's reaction was, "Man! That makes me *want* to tell the truth!" Looking back on your childhood, what might have motivated you to obey more than you did?

AIMING FOR A HIGHER GOAL

Have you ever heard how horses were trained to carry the kings and queens of Europe? Several thousand horses would be observed, then two or three were chosen to be trained. The instrument used to train them was a whistle. For weeks the trainer would blow the whistle one way and the horse was taught to respond by stopping. The trainer would then blow the whistle another way, and the horse was taught to go straight ahead at a steady gallop. The trainer would make yet another sound with the whistle, and the horse learned to slow down to a walk. After several months the horse had learned numerous commands. When it seemed the animal was completely obedient to the trainer's whistle, the horse would be put in a corral for two days and was given no food and very little water. At the end of the two-day period, a large trough of food was set out in the pasture where the smell of the food would blow back toward the corral. When the trainer could tell that the horse had smelled the food, he would open the gate. Of course, the horse would immediately run at a full gallop right for the trough. When he was halfway to the trough of food, the trainer would blow the whistle for the horse to stop. If it failed, it was taken through the training process one more time. If the horse did stop, it would go on to carry the kings and queens of Europe.[5] Discipline is a long-term investment requiring a lot of groundwork and preparation, but the outcome will be significant. In essence, parents are training their children for the King's service. When we are faithful trainers, our children will be ready when the King of Kings calls them. Can you think of a higher aim?

A parent's prayer . . . Help, Lord! Actions lead to habits which lead to character—I need to get organized and work on a training strategy while there is still time! Learning about actions, attitudes, respect and responsibility remind me of how much is lacking in my own life. I hope it's not too late for You to make those changes in me. Help me to be a good leader and listener as we work together to develop new guidelines and boundaries. Our families were so different that it gets pretty tense when we start talking about rules and all. Give me the grace that You have when I am trying to make a point. We need a clear strategy for each one of the children—and that's going to take time we haven't ever carved out before. As I list them, please bring to mind some ways I can begin to apply these principles this week. I am excited about all You are teaching me, and how it will lead my children closer to You.

DISCUSSION QUESTIONS

1. What are some benefits of setting age-appropriate behavior goals for each of your children?

2. Which area of training is your strongest: respect or responsibility? What can you do to strengthen the other?

3. Share an example of a time when it would have been beneficial to have guidelines and boundaries established *before* they were needed. How would it have helped you? Your child?

4. With which age range of children do you find it most difficult to communicate? What can you do to become a better communicator at this stage?

5. Why is it important to provide consequences for both obedience and disobedience? Describe how you are applying that principle with your children.

11 } A Toolbox of Tips

*"Do your best to present yourself to God as one
approved, a workman who does not need to be ashamed and
who correctly handles the word of truth."*
—2 Timothy 2:15 NIV

Dear Mommy and Daddy,

I hear you say you don't understand two-year-olds, so let me explain. When I'm in my high chair and I say "up" it really means "down." Or sometimes it means, "I don't want milk, I want juice," unless you give me juice in the first place. Then I want milk. When I say "out" and you open the door for me, the reason I throw a fit is because I want to stay in, unless I can go outside naked. I really don't like to go for walks if I can't ride in the stroller, unless you put me in the stroller. Then I want to walk or else be carried, or maybe scream a little. Oh, and one more thing: When you ask, "Do you have to go potty?" and I say "No," it really means, "Yes." But I like to wait to tell you about it in the car or at the market. I hope that explains everything.

Sincerely,
Your beloved two-year-old[1]

Just another testament that discipline can be a battle of the wits, requiring a miltitude of resources! If you are going to build something with much detail, you will need a wide assortment of tools—maybe a hammer, a saw, some pliers, or a miter box. If you want to be ready for the wonderful ones, the terrific twos, the tireless threes, the fabulous fours (and so on), you will not only need a strategy for discipline but a "toolbox of tips" to help you stay at least one step ahead of your child! Once you identify your guidelines and boundaries and communicate them clearly to the child, you must wait for their response before choosing the appropriate consequence—or "discipline tools" that will build up the quality you are aiming to train.

TOOLS FOR REINFORCING OBEDIENCE

For sin shall not be your master, because you are not under law, but under grace. (Rom. 6:14 NIV)

As a boy, Martin Luther's father was known to be a harsh disciplinarian. His dad beat his siblings and him with a board that was kept hanging where the children could see it—a constant reminder that he would anxiously punish them the moment they fell out of line. After studying the book of Romans as an adult, Luther began to grasp God's grace and decided to give his own children a better idea of what God is like. Instead of a board, he placed an apple where all could see it. Its purpose was to remind his children that their father was more anxious to catch them doing something good and reward them, than to catch them doing something bad and punish them.[2] We want our children to understand the difference between what they do and *who they are*. We want our teachable moments to stimulate appropriate behavior—and to show our pleasure over proper behavior, strengthening good responses in the future.

Praise Performance: "Let another praise you, and not your own mouth; someone else, and not your own lips" (Prov. 27:2 NIV). Like a drill sergeant points out every minute error made by his squad, or the border patrol waits for an illegal alien to cross the line, some parents wait for a child to make one wrong move. If you want to encourage a child to obey, praise her when she does! This moves discipline from a defensive to an offensive mode. Examples: "I like the way you obeyed the first time" or, "I'm proud of how you shared with your sister," or, "Your kind voice is as warm as sunshine!"

Good going!
You're really working hard.
You are very good at that.
You've been practicing!
You did well today.
Keep it up!
I knew you could.
I like the way you . . .
You are doing beautifully.
I like it when you . . .
Super!
You remembered!
That's a fine job.
Way to hang in there!
Great job!

Affirm Personhood: "My son, if your heart is wise, my own heart also will be glad; and my inmost being will rejoice, when your lips speak what is right" (Prov. 23:15–16 NASB). Our children must know that their identity and our acceptance are not based on their performance. Affirmation is different from praise because it focuses on the *person* rather than performance alone. "I love your sweet spirit" or "You really showed courage today," leaves a strong impression about the child's value to her parents and to God. We should avoid phrases such as, "You are a bad girl" or "You liar" because God doesn't base our identity or His acceptance on our performance. Although God hates sin (performance), He loves His children (personhood).

You're a winner.
You are kind.
I love you no matter what.
You're the best!
There's no one like you.
You're the greatest.
You are so loving.
I'll always be here for you.
You're awesome.
You mean the world to me.
I'm glad God gave you to me.
You're special.
You are a wonderful person.
You make me happy!
God loves you and so do I.

Offer Tangible Rewards: "The wicked man does deceptive work, But to him who sows righteousness will be a sure reward" (Prov. 11:18 NKJV). Tangible rewards can be seen, touched, or eaten: ice cream, homework passes, stickers, toys, tickets, or treats are a few examples. The proper use of these rewards is to express your pleasure *after* a period of good behavior: "You can get something from the treasure box since you sat so quietly during class." Material rewards can be overused and can train conditional obedience: "What will you give me to behave?" "I'll give you gum if you stop screaming," is an improper use of rewards! Amanda was having problems with tantrums when things didn't go her way. One of the things she wanted was a new doll. To motivate a good attitude, we made a chart dividing the days into morning, afternoon, and evening. When she made it through the morning without a tantrum, she got to place a happy face in the square. If she blew up in the afternoon, no happy face would go up. It took three weeks to achieve five days without a tantrum and get the little doll she had wanted. Over a year later, she remembered that lesson and told me she thought she might need another "attitude chart"!

Give Intangible Rewards: "By your teachings, Lord, I am warned; by obeying them, I am greatly rewarded" (Ps. 19:11 CEV). Things as simple as a hug, back rub, story, extra time alone with Dad, or playing a game are intangible ways to reinforce good behavior. For instance, "Let's do something you want to do, since you didn't interrupt while I was on the phone," or "We'll read an extra book since you finished your homework early." An improper use of intangible rewards would be giving or withholding time, attention, or affection based on behavior. Intangible rewards are *over and above* the usual acts that demonstrate your love every day. The beauty of these bonuses is that they make memories now while encouraging good responses later!

TOOLS FOR CORRECTING DISOBEDIENCE

Correct your son, and he will give you comfort;
He will also delight your soul.
Where there is no vision, the people are unrestrained,
But happy is he who keeps the law. (Prov. 29:17–18 NASB)

When I (David) was six, just before we were leaving for a family vacation, I stole a huge amount of change from my mother and hid it in a can under the back porch steps. When we got in the car, my mother gave us each a new little wallet and told us she had saved money so we could have a little to spend each day of the trip. When she reached into her purse to pull the money out, it was gone. I never told her what I had done, but God knew—and when I went back to get the money from the can, it was gone! That time, I did not receive direct correction—but many other times, my parents let me know that disobedience did not go unnoticed at our house! The discipline tools used for disobedience are not rated by effectiveness, but we will begin with the tool that is the most controversial and misunderstood—and the most difficult one to use appropriately.

Spank with Great Care: "He who spares his rod hates his son, But he who loves him disciplines him promptly" (Prov. 13:24 NKJV). Spanking is only one of many tools of correction. Some parents believe spanking should never be used, while others think of it as only a last resort. Others believe it is the only tool to be used—and used. Even those who believe spanking has a place in the discipline process struggle with the proper time and way to use it. For good reason, the Bible has more to say about this tool of discipline than any of the others:

> Do not withhold discipline from a child; if you punish him with the rod, he will not die. Punish him with the rod and save his soul from death. (Prov. 23:13–14 NIV)

> Foolishness is bound up in the heart of a child; the rod of discipline will remove it far from him. (Prov. 22:15 NASB)

> The rod of correction imparts wisdom, but a child left to himself disgraces his mother. (Prov. 29:15 NIV)

A neutral instrument. There are several verses that use the Hebrew word *shebet* (pronounced shay'bet), which means "to branch off" or literally "a stick." This suggests the use of an instrument like a switch for a rod of discipline—or rod of correction as some verses call it. There are other rods referred to in Scripture, but in the context of discipline, *shebet* is used in every instance.

The Discipline Game

Guidelines & Boundaries

Child's Response

Action Attitude

Action Attitude

Wrong Response (Disobedience)

Right Response (Obedience)

TOO LATE

HAPPY CHILD

GAIN RESPECT

LOSE CONTROL

Consequences

Consequences

Back To Beginning (Wait For Next Response)

Tools

Tools

Teachable Moments

- Spank with great care
- Allow natural consequences
- Verbalize appropriate behavior
- Ignore selected behaviors
- Call a time-out (Isolation)
- Remove special privileges
- Provide physical assistance

- Praise performance
- Affirm personhood
- Offer tangible rewards
- Give intangible rewards

A particular person. Proverbs 22:15 told us that foolishness is not just found in the heart, but bound in the heart from childhood. Foolishness is translated as "sin." Spanking is for the child who despises his father's instruction, who is always right in his own eyes, who rejects counsel, who lacks understanding, will not respond to direction, or who demands his own way. All of these can be summarized as *direct disobedience.*

A loving purpose. Spanking is used to give wisdom, to control, and keep on the path, to remove or drive foolishness from the heart, and to "save the soul."

A serious matter. This tool requires diligence, self-control, and love for the child. *Spare* means to "refuse or withhold." Sparing the rod is compared to hating the child and keeping the child's heart bound in sin. In fact, disobedience to parents is listed as a characteristic of falling away from God's truth in the last days before Christ's second coming: "For men will be lovers of themselves, lovers of money, boasters, proud, blasphemers, disobedient to parents, unthankful, unholy, unloving, unforgiving, slanderers, without self-control, brutal, despisers of good, traitors, headstrong, haughty, lovers of pleasure rather than lovers of God" (2 Tim. 3:2–4 NKJV).

A practical application. We decided the most practical rod of correction for us was a light, wooden spoon or a thin switch from a bush, but we tried a fly swatter and a plastic spatula at other times. Going to get the spanking spoon helped us avoid impulsive actions. When our kids still wore diapers, we placed the swats on the soft, fat spot on the back of the thigh. When there wasn't so much padding, they were applied to the bottom! Part of our discussion included our model for obedience: "Did you obey immediately? Without complaint? Completely? One swat was received for each issue that applied. If they weren't honest or purposely deceived us, they received an extra swat. The consistent use of this tool made spankings less necessary and frequent. We don't spank anymore, but we do have a commercial-size plastic spatula named "Big Brother" that serves as a good reminder!

Pre-Spanking Checklist

Never appropriate from 0 to 7 months (no direct punishment, regardless of behavior!)

Generally, not necessary from 8 to 14 months (consistent, persistent distractions and diversions are usually enough).

Most effective first direct punishment from 15 to 24 months for the child who revolts.

Less frequently used from 9 to 12 years; rarely used after age 12 because other tools are more effective.(See Appendix D for age-appropriate strategies and tools.)

Use when intent is willful, direct disobedience or defiance.

If your anger is out of control, don't use this tool!

Use a switch or wooden spoon (goal: painful memory without permanent marks).

Predetermine the number of swats and where they will be placed (back of leg or bottom represents turning the back on obedience).

Explain why you are spanking: "I want you to remember that it hurts when you disobey."

After genuine tears, affirm the child and assure of your love.

Move on with your day—it's over.

Allow Natural Consequences: "He will die for lack of discipline, led astray by his own great folly" (Prov. 5:23 NIV). Another way to say this is, "Let nature take its course." Natural consequences allow circumstances to evolve in order to train children to obey. This works well with responsibility issues like toys left outside, oversleeping, and forgetting lunches. If a child leaves his toy car in the yard after being warned to put it away, leave it in the yard, even if it gets ruined. If you always intervene when they lose their new tennis shoes, forget their homework, or break a neighbor's window, you will be reinforcing irresponsibility or disrespect. Allowing your child to reap what she sows provides an indirect form of correction that you can follow up with direct instruction.

Enforce Logical Consequences: "For even when we were with you, we used to give you this order: if anyone will not work, neither let him eat. For we hear that some among you are leading an undisciplined life, doing no work at all" (2 Thess. 3:10–11 NASB).

Parents do not intervene with natural consequences. With logical consequences we *do* intervene. At times natural consequences are too costly. An expensive bicycle left in the rain can "disappear" for a specified period of time. If your child steals a candy bar from the store, you may need to take them back to pay for it. A used "cheat sheet" in your daughter's backpack may need to be turned in to the teacher. One of our personal favorites is if you have to do one of your child's jobs, they have to do one of yours (and yours should be much harder than if they had just done their own!). This tool, when used consistently, trains children to think before they act and consider the inevitable consequences first.

Verbalize Appropriate Behavior: "Instruct a wise man and he will be wiser still; teach a righteous man and he will add to his learning" (Prov. 9:9 NIV). Parents waste energy telling kids what *not* to do. "Stop yelling." "Don't run." "Don't color on the walls." "Don't put your feet on the couch." Young children don't always know the alternative behaviors to our negative correction. While behaviors like this need to be amended, it doesn't have to be done in a negative way. Your correction can become a time of instruction. A successful approach is to tell children what they *should* do. "Use an inside voice." "Make your feet walk." "We color on the paper." "Your feet go on the floor." This tool has come in handy many times over the years. When the boys were spitting at each other, it worked great: "You can spit when you brush your teeth." When somebody says, "poop head" at the table, nonchalantly say, "When you want to use bathroom words, go to the bathroom." It kind of takes the fun out of it when you acknowledge that there might be an appropriate place for such things! Positive statements communicate the behavior you are looking for and sound much nicer. It works well with spouses, too!

Discuss, Explain, Command, and Warn (Once!): "Reproof is more effective for a wise man Than a hundred blows on a fool" (Prov. 17:10 NKJV). When he was three, Blake hit his baby sister as he swung his toy lawn mower in the air. I explained that the mower belonged on the grass and Amanda could get seriously hurt if he swung it again. He remembered for a while, but started swinging it again (not in defiance), so I moved to a command: "Keep the lawn mower on the grass," and a warning, "or we will put it away." The final step would be to enforce a logical consequence if disobedience continued (willful or irresponsible). Later you could discuss again, "We had to put the lawn mower away yesterday because you couldn't keep it on the grass," or "I was so proud that you remembered to keep your lawn mower on the grass after we talked about it." Commands and warnings only work if action follows immediately. Counting 1-2-3 is just a math lesson unless the child knows another tool will be used if he hasn't moved by number three!

Ignore Selected Behaviors: "Everyone should be quick to listen, slow to speak and slow to become angry, for man's anger does not bring about the righteous life that God desires" (James 1:19–20 NIV). Some behaviors—like sibling squabbles, whining, and tantrums—are aimed at getting a parent's attention, or stirring up their tempers! Certain words and actions may be tested out just to see how you will react. Knowing when to ignore and when to intervene is definitely an art that must be perfected. Claudia Arp teaches parents to "major on the majors and minor on the minors."[3] *Minors* are the things that probably won't matter ten years from now. *Majors* are behaviors that may become character issues in the future. For example, disrespectful, crude language or dangerous, destructive behaviors should not be ignored. Choose another tool that will communicate that these should not be repeated again!

Call a Time-Out (Isolation): "Brothers, if someone is caught in a sin, you who are spiritual should restore him gently. But watch yourself, or you also may be tempted" (Gal. 6:1 NIV). Removing the "clown" from the "audience" gives a child time to settle down, consider what has been done, or be restrained from inappropriate play (e.g., biting). A playpen, corner, or "thinking spot" can be used at home or away. Laying their head on a desk or having a silent ride in the car are other forms of time-out. If behavior is extremely disruptive, complete removal from the scene may be necessary. The amount of time needed varies by age, disposition, and severity of the offense. Be careful—for some children, being sent to their room is a reward. What about the child who won't stay in time-out, or never changes his behavior? Initially, you may need to use other tools to train what time-out means. It may take physical assistance (below) or spanking to communicate that time-out means staying in a specified place until excused. The tool of *ignoring* is used with the tool of time-out. If the child keeps pulling your attention in his direction, he has not experienced isolation at all. Observing siblings or friends having great fun—and your extra attention—often motivates the offender to redirect her behavior in order to rejoin the group. Once time-out is over, she should be welcomed back with positive words that encourage a better pattern. When isolation has been trained correctly, "Do you need time-out?" may be enough to cause a child headed for trouble to reconsider.

Provide Physical Assistance: "Do not be like the horse or like the mule, Which have no understanding, Which must be harnessed with bit and bridle, Else they will not come near you" (Ps. 32:9 NKJV). Some children need a little boost to obey immediately and willingly. If you tell your child to put away her toys and she doesn't move, you might ask if she can do it herself or if she needs "help." If she does not move, calmly place your hand over hers and squeeze just enough as you both pick up the toy to make your kind of "help" uncomfortable. She will probably prefer to do it herself the next time. This is an effective tool for preschoolers who will not get up, pick up, hand over, stay seated, or come when called. Even our teenagers get moving when I offer such help on the count of three!

Remove Special Privileges: "The judgments of the LORD are true and righteous altogether . . . Moreover by them Your servant is warned" (Ps. 19:9, 11 NKJV). The older the children get, the more they look forward to a variety of activities each day. These may include reading with parents, watching a television program, riding bikes, etc. This tool is the opposite of intangible rewards, which can train obedience. Removal of a special privilege is a potent form of correction when it has been thought through ahead of time. Following through on this is difficult, but so instructive! "The television stays off until you finish your homework." "You may not use my scissors because you did not return them." "We will have to leave because you did not obey." Be sure you are ready and able to enforce what you remove, especially if the privilege you take away penalizes the whole family.

One Parent's Response

Someday when my children are old enough to understand the logic that motivates a parent I will tell them: "I loved you enough to ask where you were going, with whom, and what time you would be home. I loved you enough to be silent and let you discover your new best friend was a creep. I loved you enough to make you take a Milky Way back to the drugstore (with a bite out of it) and tell the clerk, 'I stole this yesterday and want to pay for it.' I loved you enough to let you see anger, disappointment, and tears in my eyes." Children must learn that their parents are not perfect. "I loved you enough to let you assume the responsibility for your actions even when the penalties were so harsh they almost broke my heart. But most of all, I loved you enough to say 'no' when I knew you would hate me for it. Those were the most difficult battles of all. I am glad I won them, because in the end you won something too."[4]

A parent's prayer . . . Dear Father, You have probably wanted to literally spank me so many times. I am so grateful that You have cared enough about me to allow consequences to follow my defiance and rebellion—Yet you have not punished me anywhere near what I have deserved. You have blessed and rewarded me—and affirmed me—and used me when I really don't deserve it. Help me show this kind of compassion with my own children. Make me courageous enough to choose the right discipline tool at the right time, and to bypass another when a different one will train a lasting character quality. I really need to use "Verbalize appropriate behavior" more often—I have definitely used the negative too much! Once again, I am awed at how specifically Your word speaks to my daily challenges. As I explore it with You, give me new insights that will train me as well. Thank You, Lord!

DISCUSSION QUESTIONS

1. Which of these tools of discipline are you already using? Describe another successful tool you use that was not mentioned.

2. Which tool(s) for obedience do you need to exercise more consistently (or differently)?

3. Which of the following reaction traps do you fall into most often: reminding, coaxing, threatening, or excusing? What can you do to recognize and avoid this trap?

4. Name some situations where you can give your child the freedom to select between two or more appropriate choices.

12

Winning the Discipline Game

*"Let us examine and probe our ways,
And let us return to the LORD."*
—Lamentations 3:40 NASB

Three words dads like me dread are "Some Assembly Required"—especially since I've had to assemble two of everything for our twins! I'll never forget buying their first two bicycles. Elaine and I decided to team up for the project. I chuckled as she read the entire instruction manual, then systematically laid out every bolt and screw. Why would I need the instructions—what was the big deal about putting together a couple of wheels, a seat, and a handlebar? Guys tend to get a little competitive—and it appeared that I was ahead of her at first. But in the end, she was trying to help me get the chain in place after her bike was ready to go! What's wrong with this picture?

You can have the greatest character blueprint, the finest strategy, the highest-quality materials, and a workshop full of tools—but how many parents press ahead with character building and discipline without ever stopping to consult the instructions God has given us in the Bible? Periodically, it is important to evaluate how effective your training has been. Couples should share feedback (during teachable moments!). Adjustments are part of every parent's learning process. Four questions will help you judge how successful your training has been and should be answered each time you respond to your child's obedience or disobedience.

WHAT DID I TRAIN?

"Let the wise listen and add to their learning, and let the discerning get guidance." (Prov. 1:5 NIV)

Whether or not you are conscious of it, your children are being trained—either to obedience or disobedience, respect or disrespect, responsibility or irresponsibility. Even with a character goal in mind, it is possible to produce the opposite effect of what you desire. Let's play back what happened the last time you told your child it was time to go to bed.

> MOM: I said it's time for bed. (No response.)
> Do I need to get the spanking spoon? (No response.)
> Okay, I'm going to count to three. (No response.)
> One, two, three . . . three and a half . . . do you hear me?
> CHILD: Were you talking to me?

If that sounds all too familiar, consider what you really trained. First, you taught that she could keep playing for quite a while before you'll take any action. Next, she learned that parents take a long time to count to three. Finally, you insured that she would probably avoid a spanking by pretending she's deaf. Was that the goal you had in mind? Don't feel too bad—you would get a big kick out of watching a videotape of us too! Training actually continues after each incident. If the child obeyed, did you comment about it? Did you acknowledge how much his immediate obedience will make a difference in the future? After disobedience, could your child specifically communicate what he did wrong? Did you seize the teachable moment to clarify the proper behavior? Even in the midst of punishment, instruction goes a long way to prevent similar problems in the future.

DID I EXASPERATE MY CHILD?

A kind answer soothes angry feelings, but harsh words stir them up. (Prov. 15:1 CEV)

Steve Farrar told a story about a father who reached his limit with his children's rowdiness on a family car trip. After threats and warnings, the inevitable occurred. He pulled the car off to the shoulder, roughly removed the guilty party from the backseat, and administered a popular tool of discipline heartily with the harsh warning: "I don't want to hear one word from you for a full hour—not one word!" The child must have believed his father's threat because he sat in total silence until an hour had passed. Finally, his quiet voice came from the backseat: "Can I talk now?" His father agreed, feeling pleased that his son had finally complied with his instructions. "You know when you pulled the car over back there and spanked me? Well, my shoe fell off but you told me not to say a word."[1] How many times have we corrected our children in anger or with undue harshness, only to find that our efforts backfired on us? Ephesians 6:4 warns parents about "provoking" children to the point that they lose heart. Discipline aims to shape the will, but correction must not crush the spirit.

Nonverbal Offenses

You can provoke your child to despair without saying a word or lifting a hand. Your facial expression of scorn, irritation, or disgust—or body language communicating tension, trembling, or turning away, are picked up like radar by even the youngest of children. Giving your child the "cold shoulder" or forcing them to grovel for forgiveness is an assault to their personhood that can destroy your relationship.

Verbal Offenses

Every parent fails in this area at one time or another, but angry parents are more likely to produce angry children who in turn become angry parents. Hostility, rudeness, and cursing tear down the child's identity and build up animosity toward you.

Physical Offenses

You offend your child when you lash out in anger or if you haphazardly slap them. There is a fine line between spanking and physical abuse that is very easy to cross over. Parents who were abused during childhood often repeat inappropriate use of anger. The scars may be invisible, but may prove indelible. If you fit this profile, seek help now to destroy this destructive generational pattern. God wants to mold healthy responses in both parents and children. Work on your strategies. Choose your words carefully. Practice ahead of time—and be quick to ask forgiveness when you sin against your child.

IS MY CHILD'S SPIRIT OPEN?

A cheerful heart is good medicine, but a crushed spirit dries up the bones. (Prov. 17:22 NIV)

Gary Smalley addresses this issue beautifully in *The Key to Your Child's Heart*. The greater the harshness, the greater the pain a person feels inside. When the spirit begins to close, you will notice it in the body first, then the soul (mind, will, emotions) and finally from deep within the spirit. A child who is deeply offended may begin to pull away from you or resist affection. Their eyes may become downcast or they may recoil when you lift your hand to give them something. Children whose spirits have been crushed begin to withdraw physically and emotionally or become angry and reject attempts at conversation. If it goes on long enough, and the walls are not broken down, the result may be a severed relationship later.[2]

The True Test

Does your child enjoy talking with you? Can he naturally look you in the eye? Will she return your expressions of love? If not, you must take the initiative to restore an open spirit. Your tone of voice, words, and body language should demonstrate humility and gentleness—they may be met with confusion or suspicion at first. You might verbalize what you are observing about the child or ask questions that testify to your desire to understand what has gone wrong. "I notice that you seem angry (afraid, upset, etc). Can you talk about what is bothering you?" When you know how you have exasperated your child, it is important to specifically name your offense and ask for forgiveness. Your child may or may not be ready to answer immediately. This is the time to at least attempt to touch, hold, or kneel down beside your child and demonstrate your affection for them. After direct communication, older children may respond to a note expressing your deep regret over hurting them. Very often, your unspoken brokeness will melt even the iciest heart. We are still awed by the mercy and unconditional love children extend, but we must never take it for granted. Remember that God's *kindness, tolerance, and patience* lead to repentance—another good checkpoint for adults and their children (Rom. 2:4).

WAS MY CHILD REPENTANT?

> Godly sorrow brings repentance that leads to salvation and leaves no regret, but wordly sorrow brings death. (2 Cor. 7:10 NIV)

As a seven-year-old, our friend Wade was generally very obedient, but one Sunday he misbehaved all day long. That night his family went to church and his behavior was especially disruptive during the service. On the way home his father said, "I'm going to wear you out when we get home." They rode in silence the rest of the way, and when the dreaded time arrived for the spanking,

Wade's father asked for an explanation for the poor behavior. Very seriously, Wade gave an answer he has never forgotten. "Dad, Satan has control of my life!"

True or False?

True repentance is a change of heart characterized by honesty and confession—not by challenging you further. A truly repentant child will come forward with the genuine desire to amend poor behavior and attitudes. *False* repentance is crying in anticipation of a spanking, making parents laugh, or avoiding punishment with "I'm sorry and I won't do it again." That may be true, but if you remove the consequence, you eventually train your child to a false repentance. Even when they disarm you with statements ranging from horror to hilarity, carefully judge whether there has truly been a change of heart.

A Rebellious Heart

Rebellion must be counted as further disobedience. Was there whining or a verbal attack? Were there excuses or a projection of blame? These types of behavior indicate that the training process needs to be adjusted. Rebellion, unchecked, can proceed in a serious downward spiral. As Samuel warned Saul: "For rebellion is like the sin of divination [witchcraft], and arrogance like the evil of idolatry"(1 Sam. 15:23 NIV).

ADDRESSING SPECIFIC CHALLENGES

Different Temperaments

We have concluded from research and experience that a person's personality and emotional makeup come "programmed" at birth and are reinforced by parents who tend to pass down their own quirks and oddities. Do you recognize your child's temperament from the following descriptions?

Compliant. These children are generally docile, submissive, accommodating individuals who want to please. Their will is more pliant or flexible than their "strong-willed" counterparts. These are the children who may burst into tears when you gently correct them. As teenagers they rarely become severely rebellious. The downside is that these easygoing peace-lovers may be taken advantage of if they don't become assertive when necessary.

Strong-willed. These children are naturally independent, often obstinate individuals who desire control and may become rebellious without early intervention. These are the children you said you'd like to get hold of for a week, before you found yourself negotiating with one in your own home! *Parenting Isn't for Cowards* reported that about a third of strong-willed children are recognized at birth. Another third are identified by age one—and 92 percent by age three.[3] They outnumber compliant children by about three to one. As children, they are more aggressive and hardheaded. As teenagers, they are more influenced by their peer group than compliant teens. The good news is that the majority turn around as young adults and become pleasant, responsible people! Parents of strong-willed children must work harder to fulfill their unspoken need for approval and love. That means not comparing them to your compliant child! The best approach to discipline is to accept their rugged individualism, *start early,* and pray to discover a crack in their armor when their will can still be conquered.

Difficult. Yes, there is a category beyond strong-willed! Stanley Turecki identified them using nine different categories in *The Difficult Child.*[4] They are often ultra-sensitive, fearful, finicky, or irritable from birth. These are the children who can hear the slightest sound when they sleep; or must have all the tags cut out of their clothing; or demand that their shoes be retied ten times because "they don't feel right." These are the ones who may have problems adjusting to changes in routine and approaching new situations. Children who fall into this temperament category are truly not trying to drive you crazy on purpose! You must patiently and systematically desensitize and normalize their unique idiosyncrasies as part of your early discipline process.

Behavior Disorders

There are a small number of children for which nothing seems to work. True "conduct disorders" are a complicated group of behavioral and emotional problems in youngsters. Many factors including brain damage, child abuse, growth defects, school failure, and negative family or social experiences lead to the development of behavior disorders. Children with these disorders have great difficulty following rules and behaving in socially acceptable ways. They are often physically and verbally aggressive with other children and adults. They may lie, steal, destroy property, and misbehave sexually. They tend to fear and distrust adults and display an uncooperative attitude. For younger children, signs that indicate the need for a professional evaluation include: marked fall in school performance or poor grades in school despite trying very hard; extreme worry or anxiety shown by refusal to go to school, difficulty sleeping, or refusing to take part in normal childhood activities; hyperactivity or constant movement beyond regular playing; persistent nightmares; persistent disobedience or aggression (longer than six months with no progress); and extreme opposition to authority figures. Behavior therapy and remedial education may be needed to devise special management in the home and school. The most effective and efficient approach is to concentrate on desirable replacement behaviors rather than the child's inappropriate behavior. Treatment may also include medication, especially for those with difficulty paying attention and controlling movement, or those with an associated depression. Parents may need a consistent support group—and do need the intercessory prayer of Christian friends. The good news is that early, ongoing, and comprehensive management can help them adapt to the demands of adolescence and adulthood.

Whining

Just the other day, I (Elaine) observed a little girl and her tired mother in the checkout line. Several times she whined, "I want some gum . . . I want some gum . . ." Each time her mom said "No." Next she began moaning, "Take me to Lauren's house . . . *Take me to Lauren's house* . . ." A little more irritated, her mom said "No" again. Finally, the child tuned up for her last offensive move. "If I can't go to Lauren's house, then I want some gum." The mom sighed and threw a pack of gum on the counter. What did she just train? Whining is a very annoying habit that can persist into adulthood if it is not nipped in the bud. Children learn to whimper, beg, or drone on early—especially if it gets the desired result! Begging over and over needs a new guideline—*ask one time*—and a new consequence—or *you will get an automatic "No."*

Before correcting a child about whining, make sure you truly listen and respond as quickly as possible. Little ones do not understand why they are expected to answer the first time when they have to call you five times before you answer. Use puppets to demonstrate how irritating whining is to the listener. (Remember our character, Waldo the Whiner?) If your child begins whining later, look around quizzically and say, "Do I hear Waldo? Tell Waldo that I will only listen to a nicer voice." From that point on, do not respond until the voice quality changes. If you will apply this principle consistently and early on, you can extinguish a habit many adults need to break as well!

Tantrums.

These violent outbursts can make parents feel even more out of control than their hysterical child! Tantrums are most common during the toddler stage when children do not have the vocabulary to express their frustration and anger. Some parents "cave in" and give their child whatever will stop the screaming and kicking. Even if they don't give in, the child may still "punish" them with further outbursts. Usually, parents should literally walk away from the scene. You cannot reason a child out of a full-blown tantrum. Parents can become so distraught that tantrums actually escalate. Sometimes ignoring is the wrong tool—if a child is hurting herself or her surroundings. They may need to be restrained until they unwind. Most out-of-control children are very frightened on the inside. We struggled through this phase for nearly two years before we finally discovered the secret of breaking their cycle: "Don't get sucked into the tornado" and "Remove the audience from the clown." Within one month of consistently applying this advice, our "clown" decided it wasn't much fun performing for an empty room. During a more neutral time, we recalled how bad it felt to lose control and practiced more appropriate ways to protest the next time.

Biting.

Biting is not uncommon among toddlers, but is one of the quickest ways to alienate one parent from another! A limited core vocabulary predisposes children between eighteen and thirty months to express their frustration or loss of control in aggressive, physical ways. They are just learning to share, take turns, and interact in a group. They can't identify or verbalize when they feel ignored, teased, or jealous of another child, so they express their strong emotions with a determined push or a juicy bite! Otherwise mild-mannered parents can become quite unreasonable when their child is the victim of a two-foot-tall "psycho." They can't imagine that their child is equally capable of inflicting teeth marks if someone pushes them farther than their temperament or vocabulary can tolerate. The technique of biting back to "show them how it feels" does not train a child toward appropriate behavior— and there are enough health risks to make this tool undesirable. Rather, respond immediately—with no warnings—by removing the biting child from the scene (and any object that contributed to the incident) and isolating them within a playpen, crib, or baby gate. A brief, consistent statement like "Atchisons don't bite" or

"Stop biting" is in order. There is no need to yell or yank the child—emotions are high enough already! Give attention to the child who was bitten. Let the guilty party see that biting does not get them toys or attention and there will be no toys or attention for those who can't control themselves. When the child is calm again, help him or her verbalize "sorry" to the other child. Encourage a hug or high five for reconciliation. Teach him assertive words (or phrases) like "Stop that" "My turn" or "Share please." Do not leave toddlers unsupervised if at all possible. Later, parents and teachers should look for patterns that might explain aggressive behavior—When a bigger child takes a toy away? When another child pushes them? When a smaller child is getting more attention? Insights like these will provide clues that can help you know where training or new vocabulary words are needed to prevent future eruptions.

Sibling Struggles.

Sibling rivalry is as old as Cain and Abel. You may remember crying, "I'm telling Mom!" or "She hit me first!" It seems the ones who know us best also know which "buttons" will set us off. In fifth grade, Amanda was asked to write a paragraph about a "Goliath" in her life. She wrote: "My brothers, Blake and Joel, are like Goliath to me today, because we just get mad, argue, and hurt each other. My brothers pick on me like little scabs on their arms." Different temperaments, personalities, and birth orders set up the conditions for competition, antagonism, and a contest of wills. Though quarrels and squabbles are typical, they don't have to become the rule. Teachable moments provide opportunities to instruct about resolving and avoiding conflict. But don't expect to train brotherly love when you're in between wrestling brothers or hair-pulling sisters! Many disagreements are aimed at getting your attention. As much as possible, keep out of the middle of pointless arguments. If they escalate into physical or verbal assaults, use a discipline tool that reinforces that family members will not be allowed to tear each other down. There may need to be a cooling-off period. Squabblers can spend time alone preparing to express only *their* part in the fight when they are brought back together. Specific verbal expressions like "I'm sorry for _____" should be required. We believe a sincerely apologetic heart often follows the *habit* of a verbal expression of regret. At our house, the siblings-at-odds may write a paragraph to "build up" each other. Other times we make them prove that they can peacefully coexist while working together on an extra household job. That is usually much worse than if they had avoided conflict in the first place! Every now and then we see glimpses of hope that our children will one day be *consistently* close friends.

READ THE INSTRUCTIONS

In the early day of the automobile, a man's Model T Ford stalled in the middle of the road. He tried making adjustments under the hood, then cranked some more. He tried everything he knew, but nothing worked. After a while, a chauffeured limousine pulled up behind him. A sharply dressed, energetic man got out of the back-seat and offered his help. He tinkered with the engine a few minutes, then told the man to start it. The engine cranked right up. The man who fixed the car introduced himself as Henry Ford. He said, "I designed and built these cars, so I know what to do when something goes wrong."[5]

When it comes to the character of our children, remember that God designed and "built" them. He knows exactly what they need and what will keep them going. Psalm 103:13–14 (NKJV) says, "As a father pities his children, So the LORD pities those who fear Him. For He knows our frame; He remembers that we are dust." As you implement your character blueprint and devise your strategy and behavior goals, there will be times you'll get "stalled" in the middle of the road. That is the perfect time to return to your instruction manual knowing that God wants the best for your children too!

A parent's prayer . . . I have to admit, I want to close my eyes when it comes to examining my effectiveness as a parent. One day, I think I've got it made, then the next, the kids pull something new that makes me wonder if there's any hope for the next generation after all! Why does everything have to be so complex? I'm glad You realize the uniqueness of each one of the children. They each respond so differently. Even the hardest one to handle is really so fragile inside. Why do I end up losing my cool so often? I want them to know how much I truly love them—maybe that is how they will learn repentance. My questions always outnumber my answers. Thank You for being such a gentle and humble teacher.

DISCUSSION QUESTIONS

1. Respond to the statement: "Rules without relationship result in rebellion."

2. Which of the four diagnostic questions are most applicable to your family at this time?

3. In what ways do you offend your children most?

4. Is your child generally repentant or rebellious?

5. Is your child's spirit open to you today?

Part Four:

Developing Your Heritage

———————Do you have any pictures of your children? Most parents have albums full—or at least boxes or stacks filed away! Our parents both have a family collage in their homes, documenting several generations of relatives. The murals include many early photographic images—almost too blurry to make out. In the nineteenth century, photography was restricted only to a few professionals because it required large cameras and glass photographic plates. In 1859, Charles Baudelaire dismissed the photograph as "a trivial image on a scrap of metal." However, during the first decades of the twentieth century, the introduction of roll film and the box camera brought photography within the reach of the public as a whole. Today there are even digital cameras that can edit the photograph to make it better than reality! Most people agree with the visionary George Eastman, that a photographic notebook is "an enduring record." Photography is a technique of generating permanent images on sensitized surfaces. Light is the essential ingredient in photography. Developing photographic negatives requires meticulous discipline and patience. In a dark room, you can't see anything on the paper at first. After applying the proper photochemicals, an image begins coming into focus. Hopefully, the finished product is a clear representation of the subject the photographer was trying to capture.

The process of your child's spiritual development is something like the science of photography. Most parents desire to present their children with a clear image of God that will capture the child's attention and become etched in their heart as an "enduring record." Children are like "sensitized surfaces," with hearts that are ready to absorb biblical truth. As in photographic development, the key ingredient is *light*. Jesus said, "I am the light of the world" (John 8:12), then He went on to say, "You are the light of the world. A city set on a hill cannot be hidden. Nor do men light a lamp, and put it under the peck-measure, but on the lampstand; and it gives light to all who are in the house. Let your light shine before men in such a way that they may see your good works, and glorify your Father who is in heaven" (Matt. 5:14–16 NASB). Spiritual training is not reserved only for professionals. God wants to equip every parent with the tools to help their children know Him. From birth, children are unconsciously compiling a "photographic notebook" containing images of God snapped from everyday experiences. What does your family album look like? When it comes to a spiritual heritage, how many generations are in the picture? These final chapters will help you begin to build a strong family heritage that will shape generations to come. Let's work in the darkroom a while, and expose some of the memorable images God wants us to develop and imprint in the lives of our children.

13 | What's on Your Canvas?

"I will most gladly spend and be expended for your souls."
—2 Corinthians 12:15 NASB

A teacher asked her group of first graders to draw whatever they wished. She came around and saw little Frankie busy at work. She asked, "What are you drawing a picture of?" Frankie responded without hesitating, "I'm drawing a picture of God." The teacher, knowing her theology, said, "Well, Frankie, no one has ever seen God . . . no one knows what He looks like." Without looking up, Frankie said with a frown, "Well, they will when I'm finished." All of our children have a picture of God in their minds. In Stuart Hampel and Eric Marshall's *Children's Letters to God: A New Collection,* we are given a glimpse into some of their ideas and perceptions.

Dear God: Are you really invisible or is that just a trick? *Lucy*
Dear God: Thank you for my baby brother but what I prayed for was a puppy. *Joyce*
Dear God: If you watch in church on Sunday I will show you my new shoes. *Mickey*

Dear God: It is great the way you always get the stars in the right places. *Jeff*

Dear God: What does it mean you are a jealous God? I thought you had everything. *Jane*

Dear God: I'm doing the best I can. *Frank*[1]

A Work in Progress

Have you ever attended an unveiling ceremony? A new painting is displayed with a cloth covering it until the guests arrive at the exhibit. Anticipation builds as everyone waits for the moment when the artist's creation is revealed. Whether we realize it or not, we are painting a picture of God for our children from the time they are born. Parents are like mirrors, providing a child's first glimpses of what God is like. However, when it comes to portraying an image of God for our children, there is no unveiling ceremony where the completed painting is presented. Instead, our image of God is like a mural—a work in progress while our children watch us add more detail every day. If your canvas were exhibited today, what would it look like? Have you painted a warm and lovable Creator, or a cold harsh Critic? Does your composition reveal a tender, caring Father, or a rough, distant Caretaker? How big is the God you've drawn? Is He big enough to do the wonderful, the impossible? God's plan is that His message would be passed on from generation to generation through the family. Parents have been assigned the task of filling up our child's "canvas" with the truth of God revealed in Jesus Christ.

> For He established a testimony in Jacob,
> And appointed a law in Israel,
> Which He commanded our fathers,
> That they should teach them to their children,
> That the generation to come might know,

Even the children yet to be born,
That they may arise and tell them to their children. (Ps.
78:5–6 NASB)

A Relay of Truth

Every spring, Blake and Joel run track. They have been blessed
with the gifts of speed and endurance. I love the atmosphere of a
track meet! Somewhat like a three-ring circus, the athletes are
spread across the field, performing events like the shot put, high
jump, and pole vault. Next come the hurdles and the track events.
There is great intensity during the quiet seconds just before the
gun goes off, and the spectators shout and encourage the runners,
whose faces strain toward the finish line. There's nothing like it!
The 400-meter relay has always captured my attention (in my
track days it was called the 440 relay). It combines speed, teamwork, timing, and precision. Each of the four runners is given one
leg of the race to complete. Two keys to winning a relay are timing and hand offs. Each runner has a designated space from which
to hand off the baton. As the first runner approaches the hand off
area, the second runner begins to run slowly, then picks up the
pace so that by the time the first runner reaches him they are in
perfect stride together. Hand offs can make or break a relay team.
Teams can have great speed, but without proper exchanges they
are destined to lose the race. Once you reach a certain point, it is
too late to make the hand off. Once you pass that line, your team
becomes disqualified. Families are like a relay team. Faith in Jesus
Christ is like a baton that must be handed off. Just like a relay,
there is a critical time and space for passing on the legacy to the
next generation. It begins at birth and continues through childhood and adolescence. After that, statistics tell us that it becomes
more difficult to lead a person to the Lord. However, with God,
nothing is impossible. You may be a perfect example of His grace
and mercy!

THREE GENERATIONS OF FAITH

In 2 Timothy 1:5 (NIV), Paul wrote, "I have been reminded of your sincere faith, which first lived in your grandmother Lois and in your mother Eunice and, I am persuaded, now lives in you also." Now that's a winning relay team! Notice the generational pattern: Timothy's grandmother transferred her faith to his mother, and Eunice passed the baton to her son. What an example and encouragement that parents—and grandparents—can impact children spiritually. Timothy's mother was a Jewish Christian. His father was Greek and likely a pagan. From all accounts, Eunice took responsibility for Timothy's faith training. Ideally, both parents should be modeling faith for their children—but it can be accomplished alone as long as God is your partner. The investment Lois and Eunice made in Timothy not only affected his life, but has shaped the faith of thousands of generations, through his impact on the early church and through his biography in Scripture. In many families, one generation may be characterized by a passionate love for Christ, while the next generation turns its back on God. What happened? Somebody dropped the baton. Looking back on your spiritual heritage, who was the most influential person in your life? Perhaps your parents dropped the baton—or your grandparents before them. God is sovereign and is always behind the scenes with substitute "runners"—sometimes coaches, teachers, neighbors, or relatives. He doesn't want your heritage to be interrupted. You may feel that you have not been running the race well before now. If that is the case, don't give up! With God, it's never too late to go back and pick up the baton.

A PARENT'S FAITH

To invite others to faith in Christ, we must understand it ourselves. Remember the Golden Rule of Parenting, "You cannot transfer what you do not have." Some Christians only generally recall how they came to know Christ. Entering into a covenant with God is compared with both marriage and adoption. Have you ever heard a parent describing the birth of their child? Most can provide comprehensive descriptions of their wedding and other landmark events, but can you verbally express your relationship with God? We are commanded to "always [be] ready to make a defense to every one who asks you to give an account for the hope that is in you, yet with gentleness and reverence" (1 Peter 3:15 NASB). How can we hope to answer our children when our own salvation has not been "worked out" (Phil. 2:12)? If you have come to know God personally, think about how you were introduced to Him and the difference knowing Him has made in your life. Paul Harvey once said, "If you don't live it, you don't believe it." It is important to verbalize your faith, but your words will mean nothing if you don't live out your faith. Our children need to see that our relationship with God is the most important priority in our lives. The vitality and authenticity of our faith will have more effect on the spiritual development of our children than anything else we ever say or teach.

One day a father was listening in while his son and his buddies were playing in the backyard. He overheard them talking—and the conversation was, amusingly, one of those "my dad can whip your dad" routines. One boy proudly stated, "My dad knows the mayor of our town!" Another said, "That's nothing—my dad knows the governor of our state!" Wondering what was coming next in the contest of bragging, he heard his own son say, "That's nothing—my dad knows God!" The father slipped away from his place of eavesdropping with tears on his cheeks. He got down on his knees and prayed earnestly and gratefully, "Oh God, I pray that my boy will always be able to say, 'My dad knows God.'"[2] Would your children be able to say, "My mom and dad know God"? It is possible that the heritage of generations may be hanging in the balance, depending upon the answer to that question.

A Child's Openness

David likes to joke that he has gone to church since before he was born! When we were expecting our twins, we talked to them, read to them—and even sang songs to them. One time we went to a concert and they "danced" so hard that people started looking at us! Even though we felt kind of silly, we would always sing the same three songs to Elaine's tummy: "Oh How He Loves You and Me," "Jesus Loves Me," and "All Things Bright and Beautiful." Joel had so many complications of prematurity that he could not be held or touched without setting off the monitors to which he was attached. Not knowing what else to do when we stood by the crib, we would sing those same three songs to our tiny baby as he struggled for life. To our amazement, his respirations would stabilize when he heard those melodies. We almost forgot about our prenatal performances until a few years later. Although both boys loved music and had learned scores of songs, at bedtime—or when they were feeling ill—they always requested three particular songs: "Oh How He Loves You and Me," "Jesus Loves Me," and "All Things Bright and Beautiful." God has created children with very sensitive spirits. The Bible confirms that young children can worship and glorify God: "Have you never read, 'From the lips of children and infants you have ordained praise'?" (Matt. 21:16 NIV). They can receive training, understand Scripture, believe, and come to Christ. Timothy was said to know Scripture "from infancy" (2 Tim. 3:15 NIV). One reason adults may doubt that little children can digest spiritual truth is that so few have been given the opportunity to taste very much! The seeds sown during the preschool years can produce incredibly mature fruit during the school-age years.

A "Heart" Defect

Baby Cody was described as "the cutest pink pumpkin" a few minutes after he was born. However, within twenty-four hours it became apparent that something was terribly wrong. He began to turn blue and was struggling for every breath, even with oxygen. When all the tests were completed, the doctors announced that the infant was born with a rare congenital heart defect. Time wouldn't take care of it. Medicine couldn't repair it. Cody would have to have a heart transplant or he would die.

As creations of God, we are made to be wonderful—"in his image"—but as descendants of Adam, we have inherited something horrible—a spirit that is "dead" to God. Every human being is born with a figurative "heart defect." The symptoms may not show up right away, but the condition is indeed life-threatening. No amount of money can buy a cure. No education or research can change the outcome. No medicine or therapy can counteract the inevitable. Children do not *become* sinners because they sin. They sin because they are *born* sinners, just like their parents! No one has to be taught to sin. It is "bound up in the heart of a child" and it is revealed as soon as they learn how to walk and talk. The only hope is a heart "transplant."

ACCOUNTABLE FOR SIN (BUT WHEN?)

Parents naturally want to help their children make the right choices. But the day will come when every person must present his life to God: "Behold, all souls are Mine; The soul of the father As well as the soul of the son is Mine; the soul who sins shall die. . . The son shall not bear the guilt of the father, nor the father bear the guilt of the son" (Ezek. 18:4, 20 NKJV). Scripture does not specify an "age of accountability," but implies there is a period of time before children can know to refuse evil and choose good. How long they are "safe," only God knows. We must continue diligently preparing their minds to receive the entire gospel when they are able to grasp it.

Who's Calling?

When the boys were almost seven, we were praying for the ability to clearly answer the spiritual questions that were coming almost daily. Joel was having trouble sleeping and extremes of behavior had become more noticeable. One day there would be constant conflict and emotional outbursts followed by tenderness and sensitivity toward the things of God. One Saturday morning, Joel was with me (David) while I was running errands. The Gulf War had begun a couple of months earlier, and he began asking questions about serving in the army. He commented, "If you are in the army there is a pretty good chance you will die, right Dad?" He asked more questions about soldiers who died without being Christians. We were pretty sure that he was under the Holy Spirit's conviction at that point. A few weeks later, on the way home from Amanda's birthday party, Joel asked Blake, "Do you ever hear God calling you?" Blake said, "What do you mean—like on the telephone?"

Elaine interrupted. "Why would God be calling you?"

In a matter of fact way, Joel said, "To become a Christian."

"Why would God call you to do that?"

"Because I'm not one," he answered bluntly.

"Why do you think you're not one?"

"Because I've sinned," he declared.

Not wanting to press the issue, Elaine suggested that he bring up the subject later with both of us.

Immediately after dinner, he asked to talk privately. The three of us talked together, highlighted Scripture, answered questions, and prayed together. He simply and clearly asked God to forgive all of his sin (naming several we were surprised by!) and offered his life to Jesus. Afterward, his first two thoughts were of whom he could call and tell, and that he needed to begin praying for God to call his brother, too. We wanted each of our children to be drawn by God, not pressured by the church or us. After Joel came to

Christ, we didn't want Blake or Amanda to make an outward commitment just to follow him or please us. We continued planting and watering day after day, while relinquishing their lives to God's loving care. Three months later, we were listening to a sermon on God's armor. Seven-year-old Blake looked up when the pastor qualified that only Christians possess it. Later that night, Blake and David witnessed a fatal motorcycle accident. The incident triggered a discussion, which led to his salvation that very night. Two years after that, God summoned Amanda in a very clear way that assured us that even some six-year-olds are ready to respond to Him.

GOD'S GREAT UNVEILING

Knowledge Leads to Learning

Parents have been given the high calling to provide an atmosphere that promotes a hunger to know God. Too many parents believe the church should take the lead in spiritual instruction. Certainly, active commitment to a local congregation is beneficial, but we must remember that the very first institution that God established on earth was the family—the church came later. We can give our child the finest education, the richest experiences, and the best opportunities, but if we don't prepare them to become disciples of Christ, we have missed everything.

Learning Leads to Conviction

You can teach a child to show reverence for God. You can teach him to identify sin and its traps. You can teach them to pursue the ways of love and peace that Jesus taught, but you cannot manufacture or force the timing of genuine conviction and sorrow over personal sin. If a child can't define *sin* or identify what sin "looks like" to him as a seven-year-old, how can they be "saved" from it? The good news is, they are probably still *safe*. When they can give you a list that sounds quite personalized, they are getting closer to true conviction! This is when God's role intensifies. Parents continue to plant and water, while His Holy Spirit is deep within, developing the root system for genuine faith.

Conviction Leads to Salvation

This phase of the process is reserved for God alone. His calling and timing are a mystery that He has chosen to keep to Himself. As we continue painting a portrait of God, we are commanded to pray earnestly until our child enters into covenant with the heavenly Father. Take courage, knowing that "The Lord is not slow in keeping his promise, as some understand slowness. He is patient with you, not wanting anyone to perish, but everyone to come to repentance" (2 Peter 3:9 NIV).

BUILDING YOUR FAMILY HERITAGE

It is a sobering thought that we are always just one generation away from "godlessness." A friend of ours went to Russia, taking advantage of the first opportunity in decades to share Christ there.

The openness of the people to the gospel, and their desire to obtain copies of the Bible was overwhelming to say the least. It was a wonderful time! As she boarded the bus to leave on her last day there, she looked out over the mob of people, their faces set as they marched through life. She felt compelled to call out a final message, and jumped off the bus and into the square. In her loudest "mother's voice" and the little bit of Russian she knew, she declared, "In the name of Jesus, I love you!" The response was shocking. The rush halted. People began looking around. Some were chanting. Others were crying. All were looking for the source of the news. A young man who spoke English shared the response of the people: "Say it again. We haven't heard that name in so many years. Say it again!" How long will the door be open before there will be no one left to tell the good news to the next generation? When you consider how you will invest your time, energy, gifts, and resources, remember that nothing compares to the lasting eternal value of the souls of our children.

The Bridge Builder

An old man, going a lone highway,
Came, at the evening, cold and gray,
To a chasm, vast and deep and wide,
Through which was flowing a sullen tide.
The old man crossed in the twilight dim;
The sullen stream had no fears for him;
But he turned, when safe on the other side,
And built a bridge to span the tide.
"Old man" said a fellow pilgrim near,
"You are wasting strength with building here;
Your journey will end with the ending day;
You never again must pass this way;
You have crossed the chasm, deep and wide—
Why build you the bridge at eventide?"

The builder lifted his old gray head;
"Good friend, in the path I have come," he said.
"There followeth after me today
A youth, whose feet must pass this way
This chasm, that has been naught to me,
To that fair-haired youth may a pitfall be.
He, too, must cross in the twilight dim;
Good friend, I am building the bridge for *him*."[3]

A parent's prayer... What a concept, Lord! I am painting a picture of You for my children. That sounds great until I consider what they see at their different ages. I asked them recently to tell me three things about You, and somehow, their picture of You is an inviting one. I know at their age, I did not see You as fully as I do today. Reveal more of Yourself to me so I can continue to paint a mural big enough for them to see You for who You really are.

DISCUSSION QUESTIONS

1. Looking back over your childhood, what was your earliest "picture" of God? How has it changed during your life?

2. If God could be portrayed on canvas as you have painted Him for your children, what might He look like in their eyes?

3. Who have you most relied on for the spiritual training of your children? Why?

4. At what stage do you see each of your children in spiritual development?

   a. Knowledge leads to learning.
   b. Learning leads to conviction.
   c. Conviction leads to salvation.

14 } The Supreme Goal

*"From childhood [infancy] you have known the
sacred writings which are able to give you the
wisdom that leads to salvation."*
—2 Timothy 3:15 NASB

Suppose you planned a long voyage around the world.
Your passports are in order. Your bags are packed; the family
arrives at the dock and proceeds to board. When the officer asks
for the tickets, you have yours, but there are none for the children. "Oh well" you say, "we'll have to go on without you." As
the ship leaves the harbor, you fondly wave good-bye to your
children. They stand frozen in disbelief that you would ever consider leaving them behind on the trip of a lifetime. For a
Christian parent to rear a child with a limited knowledge of who
God is, in essence, to leave the child behind without a "ticket."
Your children must trust Christ for themselves someday, but your
responsibility for spiritual instruction cannot be overlooked or
overstated.

I (David) grew up in a pastor's home and spiritual conversation and prayer were a natural part of life. Family activities centered around the church. I remember sitting at the dinner table,
fascinated by the stories of missionaries and evangelists who visited

our home. The Bible was central, the gospel was familiar—and of course, I knew all the answers! "Invitations" and baptisms were a weekly occurrence in our church. When I was six, I walked down the sanctuary aisle and told my father I wanted to be baptized. I had seen others go forward, and thought it was the right thing to do. Three years later, I realized I had never truly trusted Christ. My parents were surprised when I expressed doubts about my conversion. Despite their assurances, I knelt alone in my bedroom and prayed to receive Jesus Christ. After that I knew for sure that I belonged to Him.

I (Elaine) grew up in a small congregation of a different denomination. My parents were active in the leadership of the church, and I have wonderful memories of children's choir, Sunday school, and Vacation Bible School. We asked a blessing before dinner and recited bedtime prayers, but conversations were more about the church than the Lord. I knew Bible stories, but don't remember really reading Scripture until I was in high school. I believed in God and memorized all the creeds, but I thought heaven was for those of us whose good works outweighed our bad deeds. I joined the church, but never connected my public confession with the need for salvation. God has ways of finding us, even if takes a while longer! I was fifteen when I first heard someone describe a "personal relationship" with Jesus Christ. There was the missing puzzle piece—and my life has never been the same!

When we had children of our own, we didn't want our spiritual training to confuse or hinder them from discovering a living faith all their own. Before they were born, we prayed that we would have the privilege of leading them to faith in Christ. Of all the ministries we have shared as a couple, nothing has compared to the joy of praying with each of our three children as they surrendered their lives to Jesus Christ! But the task of planting seeds starts years before you ever see the flower unfold.

SHARE TRUTHS AND PRINCIPLES ABOUT GOD

God desires to take possession of our children before sin masters them. A perfect beginning point is to share what God has told us about Himself in the Bible. This expansion of knowledge naturally lends itself to questions and discussions, which precede the greatest awakening of a person's life!

God's Creation

When I consider Your heavens, the work of Your fingers,
The moon and the stars, which You have ordained,
What is man that You are mindful of him? . . .
O LORD, our Lord, How excellent is Your name in all the earth!
(Ps. 8:3–4, 9 NKJV)

Nothing compares with a child's curiosity and wonder when they discover a flower, an insect, or the ocean for the first time. What perfect moments to link the Creator of the universe to everything they see, hear, and touch. One of Blake's first words was *moon,* so we would recite, "I see the moon and the moon sees me; God made the moon and God made me." You can even inspire amazement rather than fear about thunder and lightning when you whisper, "Listen! Do you hear God working out there?" When you lie under the stars, or build castles in the sand, mention that God has named every star, counted every grain—and knows the number of hairs on our heads!

God's Love

Let the morning bring me word of your unfailing love, for I have put my trust in you.
Show me the way I should go, for to you I lift up my soul. (Ps. 143:8 NIV)

Expressing God's love is best achieved by demonstrating devotion to your children every day. Little children delight in songs and games like "Who loves me?" always ending with "God loves you most of all!" Pique their curiosity by telling them about God's special plan for each person. Older children may begin to doubt that God still loves them when they misbehave. Assure them that nothing they can do can make God love them more—or less.

God's Name(s)

> No one is like you, O LORD; you are great, and your name is mighty in power. (Jer. 10:6 NIV)

When Amanda was young, she loved to hear the meaning of her names. If people only gave their first name, she would say, "No, what's your whole *big* name?" Understanding and knowing God is placed ahead of wealth, wisdom, and strength (Jer. 9:23–24), so we began studying the two hundred–plus names of God in Scripture. They provided a springboard for teaching our children the whole character of God. Get some adding machine paper and write as many names for God as you can recall on the roll of paper—Abba, Bread of Life, Door, Helper, Lamb of God, Rock, Light of the World . . . the visual image is rich. Many lend themselves to object lessons helping children picture what God is like. Last Christmas, we wanted something "spiritual" to do on Christmas Eve. We thought the kids might spend half an hour making a tree garland with names of God on it. Several hours later, amid tape, glitter, and markers, they had illustrated over one hundred of them and wrapped the entire downstairs with a border declaring God's "whole big name!"

God's Activity

Who is like Thee among the gods, O LORD? Who is like Thee,

majestic in holiness, awesome in praises, working wonders? (Ex. 15:11 NASB)

Chronicling God's work throughout history builds faith in His sovereignty. Scripture says His works are incomparable, perfect, and noble. Begin by telling Bible stories about the miraculous and everyday things God has done. Find action words that let your child know that God doesn't passively observe His creation. He never sleeps, watches over us, and *knows* everything! Every morning ask, "I wonder what God is going to do today?" then allow imaginations to run wild. Create "memorials" to God's faithfulness to your family. As children begin to see a pattern of His involvement in their lives, they become more inspired to seek Him for themselves.

God's Home

In My Father's house are many mansions; if it were not so, I would have told you. I go to prepare a place for you. And if I go and prepare a place for you, I will come again and receive you to Myself; that where I am, there you may be also. (John 14:2–3 NKJV)

Little children ask the most stupefying questions! Why can't I see God? Where does Jesus live? Does God have a bathroom? At age four, Joel asked, "How old was Jesus when He knew He was God?" We had to get back to him on that one! Heaven elicits some interesting conversations. When kids hear that God lives in a lovely place somewhere "up there" they form their own picture of heaven. When we were flying home after Elaine's grandmother died, Amanda watched us ascend through the clouds and asked, "Is this where Honey got out?" This opened the door for little talks about loved ones already with the Lord. It also opened a big can of worms— "Will toys be in heaven?" "Can we fly in heaven?" "Do robbers go to heaven?" Tell them, "Everyone who loves Jesus will live in heaven" until their next developmental leap: "What about people who don't love Jesus?" A series of books called *100 Questions Children Ask about God (the Bible, Angels, etc).* may help you get ready!

God's Son

> I am the resurrection and the life. He who believes in me will live, even though he dies; and whoever lives and believes in me will never die. Do you believe this? (John 11:25–26 NIV)

Children understand the father-son relationship, and any preschooler who attends church regularly can relate one story after another about Jesus' birth, friends, and miracles. Like Jesus' parables, common objects help youngsters understand His practical lessons on life. Children may not realize that Jesus is not a pretend character like Mickey Mouse or Cinderella. Tell them *who Jesus is*—not just a baby, a teacher, or a good man, but God Himself and the King of kings!

God's Sacrifice

> For he has rescued us from the dominion of darkness and brought us into the kingdom of the Son he loves, in whom we have redemption, the forgiveness of sins. (Col. 1:13–14 NIV)

School-age children become more curious about the details of the Cross. Without graphic descriptions of crucifixion, older preschoolers can understand that Jesus died—but unlike pets or bugs, He "came alive again." You could even demonstrate His *sacrifice* by offering to substitute yourself in your child's place one time when punishment is forthcoming. Connecting Jesus' death with the payment for sin requires several other concepts that can be introduced over time.

TEACH CHILDREN TO VALUE GOD'S WORD

All Scripture is God-breathed and is useful for teaching, rebuking, correcting and training in righteousness, so that the man of God may be thoroughly equipped for every good work. (2 Tim. 3:16–17 NIV)

You may feel inadequate to teach biblical concepts to a child, but you don't need a seminary degree—just a desire to keep learning and to translate four big thoughts into simple terms.

Believe It

How can people have faith in the Lord and ask him to save them, if they have never heard about him? And how can they hear, unless someone tells them? And how can anyone tell them without being sent by the Lord? The Scriptures say it is a beautiful sight to see even the feet of someone coming to preach the good news. Yet not everyone has believed the message. (Rom. 10:14–16 CEV)

Children who learn that the Bible is true can act on what it says to do. Every time you open a Bible, remind your child that its stories really happened, and God had people write them down for us. Bible-based music, books, and videos allow children to digest God's "love letter" in an entertaining way. They don't need an apologetics course to accept spiritual truth. Parents who are unsure about the validity of the Bible may have difficulty convincing an older child—and the world will present many other "authorities" from which to choose.

Know It

> Let the word of Christ dwell in you richly as you teach and
> admonish one another with all wisdom. (Col. 3:16 NIV)

Scripture memory is a powerful tool for children, who memorize more easily than adults. Kindergartners can learn twenty-six
verses while learning to read and write their ABCs (see Appendix
G). Most of our grandparents learned their alphabet that way—in
public school! Don't worry that children can't interpret all they
mean. When they hear their verses during conversations or sermons, their ears will perk up! Your job is to plant the seeds. God
will bring them to harvest at the proper time.

Love It

> Oh, how I love Your law! It is my meditation all the day. (Ps.
> 119:97 NKJV)

Children who watch their parents enjoying the Bible are likely
to receive it with the same enthusiasm. Keep your family Bible in
a central place, and allow toddlers to carefully touch the verses
you are reading. Preschool children, beyond tearing out pages,
need their own picture Bible even if they color a few pages. Young
readers need a Bible they can read for themselves. Most translations are between a sixth- and twelfth-grade reading level, but
now there are versions that second- to third-grade readers can
handle independently.

Obey It

> But the seed on good soil stands for those with a noble and
> good heart, who hear the word, retain it, and by persevering
> produce a crop. (Luke 8:15 NIV)

It doesn't matter what we teach our children about the Bible if they don't view it as the final word on living. Children should see that even parents must obey God's Word. If they question your authority, you can defer to God. Show them where Scripture supports your family rules. "Love your neighbor" means even the mean kids. "Keep your tongue from evil" includes not lashing back when others tease us. Refocusing children (and us) on God's Word is one of the best ways to reset minds and redirect actions all through the day.

INTRODUCE CONCEPTS IN THE GOSPEL

Parents, church leaders, and children's workers often debate "When can a child become a Christian?" We have found that children who receive creative, concrete spiritual instruction from their earliest days often recognize and respond to God at an early age. Rather than concerning yourself with the exact timetable, begin to systematically build the following concepts into teachable moments. Understanding them will equip your child to respond to the gospel when they hear God's voice.

Heart

> Then God said, "Let Us make man in Our image, according to Our likeness" . . . So God created man in His own image; in the image of God He created him; male and female He created them. (Gen. 1:26–27 NKJV)

Ask a child to show you their heart, and more than likely they will point to their "thumper." The outer person is easy to study now that we can examine bones, muscles, and organs using computer imaging. However, the inner person—the *heart*—is invisible. Even adults have difficulty distinguishing between the *soul* (Gk. *psuche*) and the *spirit* (*pneuma*) described in 1 Thessalonians

5:23. A graphic way to help children envision the "heart" is to draw and color a figure for them. A 3-D object lesson can reinforce the difference between the outer and inner person. God made us *earth suits* (glass jar) to live in. Filling the jar with water represents the "real you" residing inside your body. A little glitter symbolizes the *souls* that God makes wonderfully unique. A few drops of food coloring point out that God created humans alone with a *spirit* designed to communicate with Him.

Sin/Sinner

> For all have sinned and fall short of the glory of God. (Rom. 3:23 NKJV)

When you look at your newborn child, it is hard to imagine anything but innocence and purity. Two years later, there are still glimpses of heavenly origins—along with flashes of a "devilish" smile! As you identify right from wrong for your little one, you can teach a new vocabulary word that well-meaning parents dread: "All wrongdoing is sin" (1 John 5:17 NIV). The story of Adam and Eve and the Fall provoke vivid images of sin's origin. When you tell the part about disobeying God, add potting soil to the water in your jar to represent how sin mars the heart permanently. Illustrating generational sin requires extra jars to demonstrate the "passing down" of sin from grandparents to parents to children. Your child's grasp of sin is one of the landmarks required to understand the need for a Savior. Until they can personalize sin on their own, they are not ready to move forward to a complete profession of faith.

Death

> For the wages of sin is death, but the gift of God is eternal life in Christ Jesus our Lord. (Rom. 6:23 NKJV)

The loss of a pet is often a child's first experience with death. We've had a terrible history with pets. Our first cat, "Sugar," died suddenly from a heart problem. Next, we adopted two brother kittens *just in case.* "Curry" only lived seven months (electric garage door)—and three weeks later "Kramer" was hit by a car. The sense of loss was devastating for all of us. Observing another's experience with death may evoke conversations about our mortality, heaven, and eventually, about separation from God. Blake and Joel's close friend lost his mother in the first grade. At bedtime, they would feel sad that he didn't have a mother to tuck him in anymore. The concept of spiritual death will follow after gaining understanding of physical death.

Hell

> Do not be afraid of those who kill the body but cannot kill the soul. Rather, be afraid of the One who can destroy both soul and body in hell. (Matt. 10:28 NIV)

Hell is only mentioned fifty-three times in the King James Version, compared to almost six hundred references to heaven. Discernment is required about dwelling on the details of eternal destruction (2 Thess. 1:9). Images of fire, darkness, and suffering are not the wisest "motivators" to use with young children. However, preteens that haven't received Christ may not grasp the gravity of their eternal destiny without studying what Scripture says about rejecting Christ's offer to take our punishment upon Himself. Parents must be careful not to manipulate a fear-motivated response to the gospel. It is the invitation of God's grace, not the threat of God's condemnation, that makes it such good news!

Lost

> The Son of Man came to seek and to save what was lost. (Luke 19:10 NIV)

Believe it or not, we were crazy enough to adopt two more kittens after the demise of our other cats and so far, "Rascal" and "Bandit" have survived for over a year. We were extremely protective until they passed the age when our other pets died. Recently, Rascal didn't come home by bedtime—or the next morning. I began composing another LOST CAT poster in my mind. While checking the neighborhood, I remembered that God knows how separation feels. The parables of the lost sheep, the lost coin, and the lost (prodigal) son, illustrate how God plans our rescue before we are aware of our predicament with sin. Teach your child that God wants to "save" His lost children and take them home where they belong.

Grace/Gift

> For it is by grace you have been saved, through faith—and this not from yourselves, it is the gift of God—not by works, so that no one can boast. (Eph. 2:8–9 NIV)

Grace means undeserved favor or mercy, moving the focus off anything we've done—to rest on everything God did. Children need to understand that God's love took the initiative to pay for our sin. You can demonstrate how sin causes us to "turn away" from God. Act out how God reaches out for us and calls for us to return to Him (repent). A gift-wrapped box demonstrates that salvation is free, but we must accept it from His hands. At this point, we must be patient until God alerts us that our child's heart is ready for harvest.

LET THE HOLY SPIRIT WORK

Our task is to teach our child the foundational truths of the gospel. From that point, our responsibility shifts to allow the Holy Spirit to perform the task of bringing the child to a personal awareness of his need for salvation. It is dangerous to take over the function of the Holy Spirit by pressuring a child to make a decision. This kind of interference may turn a child away from spiritual matters altogether. Sensitive parents will pray that God will complete the task in His time, and that He will show them when He is truly speaking to their child's heart.

Young Samuel's biography is one of the most inspirational Bible stories for parents of younger children (1 Sam. 2:18–3:11 NASB). As a very young boy, he was already attentive and obedient enough to be aware that someone was calling him. However, he "did not yet know the LORD, nor had the word of the LORD yet been revealed to him." He heard his name being called three different times, but thought it was his guardian, Eli, the high priest. Eli finally discerned that it was God who was calling to the boy. His role was to instruct him how to respond when God called him again. "Go lie down, and it shall be if He calls you, that you shall say, 'Speak, LORD, for Thy servant is listening.' So Samuel went and lay down in his place. Then the LORD came and stood and called as at other times, 'Samuel! Samuel!' And Samuel said, 'Speak, for Thy servant is listening.'" Parents need to discern the work of God and show their children the way to respond when they are ready. But we must be vigilant, since we never know when He might call our children home.

A BRIEF WINDOW OF OPPORTUNITY

Ask Gary and Judy Darby how God works behind the scenes in the lives of our children. On July 5, 1995, four of their five children and Judy's father were killed in an automobile accident on their return from a holiday visit. Twelve-year-old Rebecca, eight-year-old Sarah, five-year-old Mary, and three-year-old John were buried with their grandfather on the same day. Only ten-year-old Gary Scott was left. He went home earlier for a baseball tournament. Asked if she blamed God for all the pain, Mrs. Darby answered, "He hasn't asked anything of me that He hasn't done Himself." "Saved" when she was eight years old, she remembers her mother showing her God's creation. She wanted to know this Creator. As a child, she wondered what she would have done for God if she had been alive in Moses' time. Now she knows what "the desert" must have been like. The Darbys taught their children to live by two questions, "Does this glorify God?" and "What would Jesus do?" Gary Darby pointed out that we are to live for God, not for parents. Scripture was the cord that tied everything together.

Weeks before the accident, Mary (age five) announced to her mother that Jesus was calling her home. The timing was odd because Rebecca (age twelve) had just related a dream about being in heaven with her grandfather, sisters, and younger brother. Although talk about heaven was common in their home, Mrs. Darby asked God why her children were obsessed with such thoughts. The night of the accident, only little John was still fighting for life. He had been homesick when his mom left to take Gary Scott back for his ball game. Now she rocked his lifeless body as he slipped away into God's arms.

After the funeral, Mrs. Darby was tormented about whether her Sarah (age eight) had known that God was calling her home. Exactly five months after the accident, Gary Darby pulled back the fireplace screen to make the first fire of the season. He remembered how his children once gathered around the hearth for evening Bible readings. In the fireplace were scraps of papers with Sarah's handwriting on them. Gary Scott knew what they were. "Mary Poppins." Sarah had been pretending to send a message through the chimney, like the one that floated up to Mary Poppins as she sat on a cloud.

As they pieced together the note covered with a second-grader's big printing, they saw that the note read, "I will be there with You, Lord, I will praise You, Lord. I will lift my words to You.

I will love You, Lord. I will praise You, Lord, and I will never leave You, Lord . . ." God had spoken to Sarah after all.

"It's future tense," her mother said. "She knew."[1] Will you seize your window of opportunity while there's still time?

A parents prayer . . . When I look back to my own childhood, I wonder how I ever found You. Now that I think about it, I suppose it was You who found me! That is a comfort to me today, because I never know if I have said enough or modeled enough for my children to accept You for themselves. I want them to really connect with You—and recognize that the Bible is more than a dusty old book with hard to pronounce names. I want them to taste and see and feel Your Spirit when they worship with us. Show me how to make You real to them—in bite sized portions they can digest. It helps to know You have been working behind the scenes all along—look what You have accomplished with me . . . thank You for finding me Lord.

DISCUSSION QUESTIONS

1. Describe your own spiritual upbringing. How intentional was your spiritual training during childhood? Adolescence? Adulthood?

2. At what age did your child begin asking about God?

3. What has been the most difficult question of a spiritual nature that your child has ever asked? How did you respond?

4. Which truths and principles about God need to be "filled in" for your child?

5. What area of valuing God's word most needs to be applied in your home?

    a. Believe it.
    b. Know it.
    c. Love it.
    d. Obey it.

15 } Shaping Young Disciples

"I have no greater joy than to hear that my children are walking in the truth."
—3 John 4 NIV

A bright student who was admitted to Harvard celebrated the event with family and friends. Afterwards, his mom dropped a word to the society editor, who in turn ran a short feature along with his photo. His dad clipped it and had it framed for his bedroom wall. Over the years, when someone noticed the hanging, the son enjoyed retelling the old, old story of the day he was accepted to Harvard. It was a sad story, as well. No one ever helped him visit the campus, enroll in classes, find the library, or attend Harvard at all! He remained oblivious to all that was available to him, and worked at a menial job all his life. He had misunderstood that admission to the university was the finish line instead of the starting point.[1]

Like being admitted to college, entering into the Christian faith is not an end, but only the beginning of a new life. Your children are going to need you to join them as they begin their journey. A new Christian is like a newborn in many ways. At first he needs intensive support and instruction to grow up in the faith. Young disciples will require more than Sunday school or church attendance to fully mature. The time will come when God will use various people to impact your developing young person, but first he needs your help to establish a life-style of discipleship.

DISCIPLEMAKING 101

Have you ever noticed how close the words *discipline* and *disciple* are? There is still a lot of training to be completed! We were fortunate to attend a church that provided a New Christian's class to help children solidify their conversion experience before baptism and church membership. After that, we were on our own. Slowly, we developed a framework for discipling our own children as they learned to take "milk" then transition to "solid food." "As newborn babes, desire the pure milk of the word, that you may grow thereby, if indeed you have tasted that the Lord is gracious" (1 Peter 2:2–3 NKJV).

DISCIPLES HAVE A NEW IDENTITY

You are not the same person you were before salvation! Does your young disciple realize this good news and how it can impact the rest of his life? God's Word says a lot about this new identity. Because you were grafted into the life of Christ, you were declared holy, dearly loved, a saint, a citizen of heaven, a son or daughter of God, and a joint heir with Him. Like a caterpillar is transformed into a butterfly, we are born a second time and emerge as a new creature (2 Cor. 5:17). The Bible calls this regeneration, or new birth.

Happy Birthday!

Just as you celebrate your child's physical birthday, you can celebrate their spiritual birthday after they have been "born again." These celebrations are especially significant for children who were young when they received Christ as Savior. Every year,

we spend an evening alone with each of our children to com-
memorate the day they became a Christian. We go to the restaurant of their choice, allow them to order anything they want,
then review God's work in their life over the past year. Our tradition is to recall the events that led up to their covenant of faith.
We also take turns sharing the development we have observed
over the last twelve months. Finally, we set some goals for the
year ahead, and present a small gift as a memorial of God's grace
in their lives.

DISCIPLES ARE BEING TRANSFORMED

Imagine the proud parents of a new baby boy! What if, two
weeks after they brought him home, the parents had to take him
to the doctor's office to get his legs—and one month later, they
had to bring him back to have his ears attached—then at the age
of two, he would receive his brain. Sounds crazy doesn't it? A
baby has everything present and programmed at birth. Unless
something is damaged or neglected he will continue to develop
and grow. In the same way, spiritual newborns already have
everything needed to grow up in the faith. "His divine power has
given us everything we need for life and godliness" (1 Peter 1:3).
At the time of salvation, God installs all of the equipment necessary for you and your children to become spiritually mature and
fruitful.

Where Is the New Creation?

If Christians have been made new creatures, then why don't
they always look or act differently? The fact is, what God has made
new is invisible to the human eye, and He has quite a bit of fin-
ishing work and detail left to complete. For now, you still live in
exactly the same *body* . . . and your *soul* can reason (mind), feel
(emotions), and choose (will) like before. However, your *spirit* that
used to be dead to God, has now become *"alive"* to God (Rom.

6:11). He has actually come and made His home inside of us! (John 14:16–17, 23). So what does He want to accomplish now?

Souls Being Remodeled

No matter how "good" a person is before becoming a Christian, they have been "pressed" into sinful patterns by sin, and the imperfect world we live in. Thankfully, God has a strategy for accomplishing this work, too: "And do not be conformed to this world, but be transformed by the renewing of your mind"(Rom. 12:2 NASB). Human effort may train the mind, but only God can *renew* it. This is a supernatural process that can't be duplicated by mere intellectual effort. Reading, studying, and meditating on Scripture are like planting God's very thoughts into our minds so that His Spirit can use them to change how we think and act.

Transformation Is Promised

God wants to mold us into the image of Christ, so others can see what He really looks like and be drawn to Him. The character blueprint you designed was drafted after first looking at God's character. Once your children belong to Him, they possess the foundation and source of every quality you picked. Happily, God will be working from the inside, while you remain active on the outside. Our hope and confidence come from Philippians 1:6, which states that "he who began a good work in you will perfect it until the day of Christ Jesus" (NASB).

GOD RENEWS MINDS AS DISCIPLES FEED THEMSELVES

Do you know a ten-year-old child whose parents still feed him with a spoon? If so, he must have a significant disability, because self-feeding is a much earlier developmental task. At first, babies depend on their parents for sustenance, but progress to spoon foods, then finger foods. Finally, they master a spoon and fork for themselves, and may even cut meat by the time they go to school.

We should find it very peculiar if a Christian goes for years—even decades without ever learning how to feed themselves from the Word of God. Instead, we are satisfied to be "spoon-fed" by pastors or speakers as long as they will accommodate us. Your growth as a Christian, and your ability to disciple your children, depends on learning how to feed yourself God's Word.

Disciples Need Daily Nourishment

A fable is told about three men who were traveling in the desert. They came upon a stranger who told them that in the night they would come upon a dry riverbed full of stones. He told them to fill their pockets and saddlebags with the stones and the next morning they would be both "glad" and "sorry." The stranger was right. They came upon the riverbed and found some stones and put a few of them in their pockets. The next morning they were, just as the man said, both glad and sorry. The stones had turned into precious stones and jewels. They were glad they had gotten the precious stones, but sorry they had not gotten more.[2] God's Word is an inexhaustible treasure full of truth—when we take the opportunity to discover it. Help your child begin the discipline of reading a passage of Scripture every day. They may want to read a chapter, or choose one psalm or proverb to explore. When you read verses together, talk about how they apply to them. This helps them begin to "digest" truth rather than just "swallowing" it. They can even underline verses that are meaningful to them. Older kids may even color-code commands (red), promises (yellow), and warnings (orange) using map pencils.

Disciples Need Weekly Feasts

On Sundays, encourage a quiet ride to church for the purpose of getting prepared to worship and hear God's Word. During the sermon, help them listen for Scripture and jot down references they hear. Let them copy key points from your notes. On the way home from church ask what they learned in Sunday school. It helps to ask their teachers for the weekly topics a month ahead of time! The "jewels" they found can be used to develop the next week's study.

Disciples Need to Build Muscle

Memorizing Scripture is like bodybuilding—eventually your work shows on the outside. If your kids want to memorize verses, have them write the Scriptures down in a specific place so they can review them every day. The next week, they can add a new verse (then record last week's reference beside it.) They won't forget last week's verse if they continue to practice it along with their new one. If they will keep reviewing each verse for six weeks, it will stay etched in their minds for a long time!

DISCIPLES WALK WITH GOD

Many years ago, a very wealthy man lived in a spacious castle near a small village. It had rooms full of treasures, gold, and silver. After months of seclusion, he entered the village and announced that he had built a giant maze on his property. The walls were very high, and the maze stretched out over several hundred acres. He said he had placed all of his treasures in the center of the maze and that anyone who could get to them could have them all. Since everyone in the village was poor, all the men packed their knapsacks, said good-bye to their families, and set out to find the treasure. Several weeks passed, and a few men came out reporting that men were dying or going insane from confusion. One young man stood near the entrance to the maze, contemplating his own attempt, when suddenly he heard a voice behind him ask, "Are you going in alone?" Startled, he turned to see an old man behind him. "No, I am afraid of going in alone. Many men have lost their lives in there, and I would surely die also." Looking deep into the young man's eyes, the old man said, "My son, I built that maze and I have the map. I know every corner and turn.

Follow me and I will lead you straight to the treasure if you stay close, and walk in my path."³

Our Companion and Guide

The world we live in is much like an uncharitable maze in which we can easily become lost and confused. When we must release our children into it, we can be comforted knowing that they will always have God as their companion. We should teach them to picture God walking along with them, sitting at lunch with them, and falling asleep with them. They will be reassured knowing that even when Mom and Dad can't be there, God is available to guide them. When we look for opportunities to share situations in our own lives where we rely on God, they will look for circumstances to call on Him. Some of the most thrilling words ever to come out of our children's mouths are how they asked God to show them the right thing to do, or prayed throughout a game, or when they were nervous before a recital. These aren't the signs of a religious system, but a significant relationship with the Creator of life. "And the LORD is the one who goes ahead of you; He will be with you. He will not fail you or forsake you. Do not fear, or be dismayed" (Deut. 31:8 NASB).

DISCIPLES MINISTER IN THE WORLD

A patient in a hospital knocked over a cup of water, spilling it on the floor beside his bed. Afraid he might slip on the water if he got out of bed, the patient asked a nurse's aide to mop it up. Hospital policy stated that small spills were the responsibility of aides, while large spills were to be mopped up by the housekeepers. The nurse's aide determined that this was a *large* spill, so she called the housekeeping department. When a housekeeper arrived, she declared the spill a *small* one, and an argument followed. "It's not my responsibility," declared the nurse's aide, "because it's a large puddle." The housekeeper disagreed. "Well, it's not mine," she said. "It's too small." The frustrated patient finally took a pitcher of water from the bedside table and poured it on the floor. "Now is that puddle big enough for you two to decide?" The argument suddenly ended![4]

Counteract a "Me-Centered" Worldview

A common characteristic of boomers, busters, and Generation X-ers is a self-centered point of reference. Even in a global society, our own world is often quite small. Just ask a child to define words like *poor, lonely,* or *sad.* You'd be amazed how many kids give responses like: "Poor means no money to buy Nike tennis shoes." "Lonely means not having anyone to play video games with." "Sad means crying because your mom won't let you go to your friend's house." No wonder their worldview is so limited—they've probably never had to observe life outside of their own safe environments. Parents seeking to shape disciples who will impact the next generation need to correct the child's picture of the world in which we live.

Imagine that the entire population of the earth could be reduced to a multinational village of just one hundred people. First of all, our village would consist of eight Africans, fourteen North and South Americans, twenty-one Europeans, and fifty-seven Asians. (We might want to think twice about our attitudes about other races if we are interested in reaching the world.) Half of the entire wealth of our little village would be in the hands of six inhabitants. All six would be United States citizens. That should remind us that those who hold the wealth are expected to share it. Only one would have a college education, and seventy of the one hundred people in our village would not even be able to read this paragraph . . . or the Bible.[5]

Promote a Sense of Calling

My (David's) mother instilled in me the hope and expectation that God would call me to do something significant for Him. We have tried to maintain a running conversation with our children to keep them alert that God uses disciples of every age for His work. Our children should grow up in anticipation of the exciting tasks God will call on them to accomplish. Rather than asking, "What do you want to *be* when you grow up?" teach them to ask God what He wants them to *do* when they get older—as Christians, they should already know who they *are!* In Ephesians 1:18, Paul prayed that the Christians in Ephesus would catch a vision for God's calling: "I pray that the eyes of your heart may be enlightened, so that you may know what is the hope of His calling" (NASB). Help them dream big—God doesn't just call pastors and missionaries. Every believer has a calling. They may be called to a vocational ministry, but any occupation or career can be considered a "mission" to which we are assigned.

Involve Them in Serving

Last spring, Blake and Joel went to Washington, D.C. with their school. They enjoyed visiting all the monuments, memorials, and sites on their agenda. Last summer all three of our children returned to the District—but the streets where they worked looked nothing like the avenues full of cherry blossoms and brand-new cars. One of the best investments we have ever made was to send our kids to work for ten days in the inner city of one of the nations most brutal locations. They joined several hundred other teens, dividing into ministry "tracks" like construction, recreation, special needs, day camps, AIDS care, homeless shelters, and creative ministries. The work was hard. The people were novel—many of the children had never seen a white person within their projects. The teens were suspicious. The little ones were starved for affection. And our kids' eyes were opened wide—God helped them personalize their image of a hurting world, and we knew they had experienced the compassion of Jesus—because the needs of His children made them weep.

Lead Outside Your Comfort Zone

Although we have always been devoted to home and foreign missions, our own experience is just beginning to develop. We started by picking out and delivering gifts to needy families at Christmastime. Children who see the excitement the simplest gifts can elicit become more grateful. Our church partners with an inner-city church in our town, so the experiences our kids had out-of-state are being brought closer to home. One of our family dreams is to go overseas on a partnership mission. The most difficult part is for parents to reprioritize spending to allow for a trip of this kind. It is exciting to hear our children's desire to share Christ on another continent above taking an exotic vacation! God wants to move us beyond the boundaries of our personal comfort, to see where He is working in the world—or in our backyard, and to join Him there for "kingdom" purposes!

No Other Plan

In his book *Dare to Share,* Roy Fish tells an imaginary story about Jesus ascending to heaven and seeing the angel Gabriel. Gabriel was interested in what our Lord had been doing on earth. Jesus explained that while He was here, He experienced childhood, obeyed His parents, did some carpentry work, and spent three years traveling and teaching and investing Himself in a handful of friends before being crucified on a cross and being raised from the dead. Jesus ended by saying that He wanted all people everywhere to know that His death on the cross was to save them from their sins so they could have eternal life. Gabriel asked, "And what is Your plan for spreading this message?" Our Lord responded, "I have left the message in the hands of a dozen or so men. I am entrusting them to spread the good news all over the world." Somewhat surprised, Gabriel exclaimed, "Twelve men? What is Your plan if they fail?" Jesus replied, "I have no other plan."[6]

Two thousand years later, Jesus' plan is still in force. While He did speak to large crowds on occasion, His primary strategy was to prepare a handful of ordinary men to change the history of the world. Two millennia have proved the effectiveness of the law of multiplication: Spend several years pouring your life into a small group of people. Walk with them, eat with them, travel with them, teach them, and give your life away for them. This is the essence of true discipleship. We can follow in His footsteps—our greatest prospects for discipleship are right under our noses!

A parents prayer... So many seeds are being planted and ideas are beginning to germinate. I pray that each child in our household will truly know You. I have seen that as an end, but in reality, salvation is only the beginning of my lifelong task as a discipling parent. There are so many truths and concepts I long for them to know. They will need to be stronger than I was at their age. I am so thankful for Your Spirit of truth that will teach them far beyond my capacity for discipleship. Thank You for directing us to a God-centered congregation, who are supporting us in our quest for knowing You. I am Your disciple and You are my teacher. With Your help, I will mentor them from what You have taught me.

DISCUSSION QUESTIONS

1. Name the individuals who have discipled you over the years.

2. What is your true identity as a Christian?

3. How has God been renewing your mind and transforming your life during the last three months?

4. What area of your life is most in need of development and discipleship?

   a. Self-feeding.
   b. Walking with God.
   c. Ministering in the world.

16 } The Ultimate Gift

> *"Arise, cry aloud in the night,*
> *At the beginning of the night watches;*
> *Pour out your heart like water*
> *Before the presence of the Lord;*
> *Lift up your hands to Him*
> *For the life of your little ones."*
> —Lamentations 2:19 NASB

Several years ago in the heat of the school prayer debate, a senator was asked to address the annual men's dinner at a local church. About 450 were present. School prayer had become a very emotional issue, and the senator began by asking two questions. "First, how many of you would like to see prayer restored to the public schools?" As far as he could tell, every hand was raised, with many "Amens!" The second question: "How many of you pray with your children every morning at home?" The silence was embarrassing. Finally, a few raised their hands—reluctantly, it seemed. The senator aptly pointed out how interesting it is that we *talk* about the importance of prayer yet actually do it so little.[1] Of all the steps a parent can follow to leave a legacy of faith for their children, prayer is at the top of the list.

PRAYING FOR YOUR CHILDREN

Job did more than talk about prayer, he prayed. He prioritized and valued his family over his career, wealth, social standing, and reputation (Job 1:1–3). One of the rewards was that his ten children still maintained close relationships, even after they were grown and out of the house (1:4). For some of us, that counts as a miracle! Let's look more closely at Job 1:5: "And it came about, when the days of feasting had completed their cycle, that Job would send and consecrate them, rising up early in the morning and offering burnt offerings according to the number of them all; for Job said, 'Perhaps my sons have sinned and cursed God in their hearts.' Thus Job did continually" (NASB). Job was obviously very dedicated to his children and extremely concerned about their spiritual development. Early in the morning he would petition God on behalf of his children during his personal worship time. His ritual provides several insights that we can draw on. Who knows—you may be the only person praying for your child. It is a responsibility and privilege we should not neglect. Job prayed for his children one at a time—"according to the number of them all." Because spending time with them was already a priority, he probably knew what was going on in each of their lives. Really knowing your children helps you become a more effective intercessor. Job knew that what happens on the inside ultimately shows up on the outside. Our prayers should cover our daily concerns for our children— health, safety, grades, and behavior are certainly worthwhile subjects to bring to God. However, we should place a higher priority on praying for our child's inner life than his outward behavior, since outer conduct begins with thoughts and attitudes.

PRAY WITH PURE MOTIVES

A mother complained to her brother about her son's failure to write home. Away at college, he had become too busy—or too uncaring—to write home. Her brother boasted, "I'll show you something about boys, Sis. I'll get him to write me a letter without even asking him to." To prove his point, he wrote the boy a short note telling him how proud he was of him. He also wrote that he knew school was expensive so he was sending $20 for the boy to spend as he liked. But he didn't enclose the money! Very shortly he received a letter from the lad thanking him for the concern—and mentioning the oversight. The uncle's prank highlighted the boy's true motivation for writing to his family.[2]

I wonder what our true intentions look like to God. The content and consistency of Job's prayers reveal his motivation for intercession. If the content of our prayer centers on performance or achievement alone, we must check ourselves to determine if we are seeking God's will or our agenda. We need to go before Him with honesty and openness, confessing our shortcomings and expressing a genuine desire to first develop a deeper fellowship with Him because of *who He is*—and not for *what He will do* for us or for our children.

Include "Listening" Prayer

A scientist and a minister were walking down a busy street in a crowded city one day when the scientist asked, "What do you hear?" The minister answered, "I hear the chatter of passing people, the noise of traffic." The scientist was an entomologist— a specialist in the study of insects. He told the minister, "I hear a cricket above all the sounds you have mentioned." He then went to a nearby office building, moved a small stone, and pointed to the cricket that had found refuge there. The minister was amazed. Then the scientist led him back out onto the crowded sidewalk. "Now watch this," said the scientist, smiling. He reached into his pocket, pulled out a quarter, and dropped it. Though the sound was almost inaudible, several people instantly turned to see where the money had fallen. The scientist remarked, "You hear what you want to hear, and what you are trained to hear."[3] Any good conversation must include listening. After you have brought your concerns to God, make yourself sit quietly for as long as you possibly can. Often the Holy Spirit will respond with an impression or a thought of a Scripture verse that will enlighten you to the next step or further prayer.

Pray Systematically

Job prayed consistently ("early in the morning") and persistently ("thus Job did continually"). Praying for our children is not a temporary measure taken during a crisis. It is a lifelong activity that we should aim to build into our lifestyle. In their early years, we both kept a separate section for each child in our journals. Elaine would write out her prayers for them, as well as the profound things they said or asked. Each year, I (David) would list specific petitions that could be revised as needed. Every day I would pray through my particular requests for each child:

> Above all things I ask You to protect Blake until the day he accepts Christ as Lord and Savior (Rom. 10:3).
> Help Blake obey us and develop respect for authority (Eph. 6:1).
> Teach him to be kind to his brother and sister and friends (Eph. 4:32).
> Help Blake to be strong and courageous in the Lord. Give him godly confidence (Josh. 1:9).
> Give him a spirit of joy and happiness (1 Thess. 5:16).

Later, we developed the 31 Daily Petitions (see Appendix F), scripture verses with one request for each day of the month. This created a guide for character building as much as for prayer. Two unexpected blessings grew out of this discipline. First, it brought specific areas of character development to our attention. Second, we told our children what we were praying for them each day.

After a while, they would ask what we were praying for on a given day, opening the door for a teachable moment.

Pray Specifically

When the blind man approached Jesus, he said "I want to see." General prayers get general answers. Specific prayers get specific answers. Vague requests do not reflect a comfortable, intimate relationship with God. Acquaintances have brief conversations that rarely get personal or have much substance. Intimate friends can talk for hours, and are willing to be open about needs, concerns, and anxieties. Sometimes we pray general prayers due to a lack of faith over previous disappointment with God. (If I don't get too specific, maybe I won't be so let down if God doesn't "come through.") Be explicit in your requests, always qualifying that you trust in God's sovereign love for your child. Regardless of His answer, He always responds, "Be anxious for nothing, but in everything by prayer and supplication with thanksgiving let your requests be made known to God" (Phil. 4:6 NASB).

Pray Expectantly

Psalm 5:3 reflects our hope as we bring our children to God: "In the morning O LORD, Thou wilt hear my voice; in the morning I will order my prayer to Thee and eagerly watch" (NASB). When we articulate our thoughts and longings to the Lord every day, we will develop an anticipation of how God is going to work throughout the day. How thrilling it is to pray for your child in a specific area and then see a change in attitude or behavior that is a direct response to your request. Model Moses' bold, extravagant request after acknowledging that he could never lead the children of Israel without God's presence—"Please, show me Your glory" (Ex. 33:18 NKJV). When your child is in a crisis, do everything you can to help—but don't forget to acknowledge your utter dependence on God by praying, "As long as I'm here, Lord, show me Your glory!"

Pray Scripture

In *Man in the Mirror*, Patrick Morley tells about seven couples, all new Christians, who started to meet in a prayer group. The results of their prayers were so dramatic that he verified their story with three separate sources. They all checked out. It seems these naive new Christians discovered a verse of Scripture and decided to claim it as a promise from God. Acts 16:31 says, "Believe in the Lord Jesus, and you will be saved—you and your household" (NIV). Among the seven couples, they had twenty-three children, none of whom were Christians at the time. Each week the couples would faithfully pray for the salvation of their beloved children. Over the course of two years, all twenty-three committed their lives to Jesus Christ![4] As we spend time meditating on God's Word, it "speaks" His will and instruction into our own life. When we pray God's own words, we agree with Him about what He has already said. We know we are praying God's thoughts. A great place to start is in the Psalms. Whatever is happening, we can see our own lives in the passionate reflections penned by its authors. God encourages us to come to Him, flaws and all—He will never turn His children away.

Praying *with* Your Children

Praying for your children may be your most significant activity during parenthood—particularly as they grow older. But it is equally important for you to pray *with* your child, if you want to shape his ability to pray effectively. Susannah Wesley spent one hour each day praying for her seventeen children. In addition, she took each child aside for a full hour every week to discuss spiritual matters. One of her training principles included teaching children to pray as soon as they could speak. No wonder two of her sons, Charles and John, were used so mightily to bring blessing to all of England and much of America![5] Praying with your children can begin when they are old enough to fold their little hands while you ask for God's blessing at meals, or tuck them into bed. If they hear you pray in a normal, conversational way, they will learn that talking to God is a natural thing to do.

Watch Your Language!

A little girl was sent to bed by her mother, and after several minutes she heard the child exclaim "Someone's been eating my porridge, too, and it's all gone!" Peeking through the doorway, the mother said, "Honey, you're supposed to be saying your prayers. "I am, Mama," the little girl replied. "I figured God was bored with hearing the same old thing, so I'm telling Him the story of 'Goldilocks and the Three Bears.'"[6] Since we want to model that prayer is a "little talk" with God, be careful to avoid spiritual clichés and confusing doctrinal words. If you dramatically change your voice or vocabulary when you pray, your child may become confused—or bored with your verbose, poetic repetitions. Instead, we need to keep our conversations with God simple and genuine.

"Pray Angels!"

When our children were tiny, we began our bedtime tradition of individually tucking each child into their bed, singing a few choruses, and praying for them. When they only used single words, we would encourage them to participate by imitating "Amen" or "Jesus." When they could use short phrases, we added more: "Thank You God," often signaled a long list coming! Without even thinking, we would pray that God would put His angels all around their beds to watch them while they slept—or minister to them if they were sick. If we ever forgot to include angels in our prayer, they would cry, "Pray Angels! Pray Angels!" We've wondered sometimes if that might explain why none of our children have ever feared the dark or closed doors.

Model Balanced Prayers

Pray for your child, then let her have a turn. This is the way to practice and develop the language of prayer. Grateful children are trained to thank God for everything. However, their prayer life will not fully blossom until we expand the scope of their conversations with God. They need to learn how to tell God how great He is (worship/adoration)—the names of God provide the vocabulary they need to say, "I love You, God, because You are my strong Rock." Parents who will model the prayer of confession and repentance are training humility before God. This is the time of the day when you can talk to your child about the ways that you might have offended them during the day. When they hear you ask God to forgive you for yelling or becoming impatient, you are raising their consciousness about God and themselves. Let them tell God about the most trivial concern that seems real to them. Communicate that He is interested in absolutely everything that concerns us. Finally, don't forget to pray for others. Intercession turns the focus from us to others. Little children have no problem thinking of a long list of significant others—from the man at the grocery store to the birdie that fell out of the nest! Starting this pattern at a young age reaps big rewards for an older child who is comfortable communicating in intimate ways. Children are never too big for bedtime—or anytime—prayer. It is usually the parent who becomes too busy in the evenings to stop long enough for conversations with their child and with God. If you keep the lines open all through childhood, you are much more likely to maintain open dialogue with your teens—now that's a motivator!

Pray Anytime or Anywhere

That is one of the great lessons my (David's) parents taught me. Sometimes we would be talking about something in the kitchen or the car and my mom would stop everything and say, "Let's pray about it now." It didn't matter if it was on the phone, in the car, or the store, we would pray! If we teach our children Matthew 28:20—"I am with you always" (NKJV)—they won't be surprised to know they can pray outside of a church pew. Amanda wouldn't think of eating a bite of food before asking God to bless it. Even when it has been awkward, we pray as a family, even in public. We can't begin to tell you all the times people have come over and commented how much hope it gives them to see that families (with teenagers!) still find prayer important.

Never Give Up

When we encourage our children to pray with us about family concerns, they will learn that God always answers our requests and meets our needs. They also learn that one can actively trust God, then "do the next thing" without fretting further. Parents should be sure to point out how God has responded—and to reiterate that sometimes His answer may be "No" or "Not yet." There have been times when finances have been extremely tight and we have asked our kids to join us to ask God for provision for our needs (versus desires—another good lesson!). Several months ago, we began praying expectantly that God would sell our house right away, since the market was "hot." It took six months—and scores of showings—before we received an offer. It was so enlightening to see how differently each person responded in prayer over time. At one point, we moved to a prayer of "relinquishment" when it looked as if God's plan was for us to be content and stay put. It was probably harder for us than it was on our children to model that prayer! When the house finally sold, it was a joy to hear our children individually thank God for blessing us with so much more than we need or deserve.

SHAPING THE NEXT GENERATION (ON YOUR KNEES)

We have discussed the importance of correcting our vision, designing our strategy, training our child, and building our heritage—and each of those has their source in our heavenly Father. Before you read this book, you may have felt that you were barely surviving the demands of parenthood. We hope you have learned that God has strategically placed you in this generation to play a major role in preserving the generation yet to come. Keep striving to raise champions for Christ, regardless of how dark the days may appear. If only we could stand back far enough to take in God's view of our planet, we would be able to see the importance of our children in the coming generation.

One "Ordinary" Visionary

George McClusky was that kind of man, though he was never famous. To our knowledge, no biographies have been written about his life. McCluskey was a man who decided to make a shrewd investment. As he married and started a family, he decided to invest one hour a day in prayer. He was concerned that his kids follow Christ and establish their own homes where Christ was honored. After a time, he decided to expand his prayers to include not only his children, but also their children and the children after them. Every day between 11:00 A.M. and noon, he would pray for the next three generations.

As the years went by, his two daughters committed their lives to Christ and married men who were full-time ministers. The two couples produced four girls and one boy. Each of the girls married a minister and the boy became a pastor.

The first two children born to this generation were both boys. Upon graduation from high school, the two cousins chose the same college and became roommates. During their sophomore year, one of the cousins felt called to go into the ministry. The other did not. He knew the family history and undoubtedly felt some pressure to continue the four-generation family legacy by going into the ministry himself, but he chose not to. In a manner of speaking, he became the "black sheep" of the family. He decided to pursue his interest in psychology and over the years, met with success.

After earning his doctorate, he wrote a book to parents that became a best-seller. He then wrote another—and another, all best-sellers. Eventually he started a radio program now heard on more than a thousand stations each day. The black sheep's name? James Dobson.[7] Without a doubt, he has been one of the most influential Christian leaders in this generation. I wonder, however, how much more God will reward an "ordinary" father who lived four generations ago? He is the real hero, for he discovered that the first place to begin shaping the next generation is on your knees.

As you consider the things that you have read in this book, will you begin painting a new picture of God for your children? Our own little world is our family, and it is hard to imagine how our children might make a difference in human history and God's kingdom. If we could only stand far enough back to see God's view, we could look down on a whole planet of wandering people who will desperately need our children to lead them in years to come. Now that's a vision to pray for!

A parent's prayer . . . Jehovah Jireh—The Lord Provides. Jehovah Rapha—the Lord Heals. I am determined to remember and celebrate the countless times You have answered prayers for me and for the children. On the other hand, I must forget hundreds of things you do for us and protect us from every day. I pray so inconsistently and with a lack of passion, considering the power You have made available to me. You have been stirring me up deep in my soul. You have renewed my heart for You and a longing for prayer that truly gets through. Give me the tenacity and vision of George McClusky to pray not only for my own children, but for future generations. Only You will really know the investment I am choosing to make, but I am standing in the confidence that You will cause it to multiply for thousands of generations! Amen.

DISCUSSION QUESTIONS

1. What role did prayer play during your childhood? What role has it played since you became a parent?

2. Is prayer more of a "last resort" effort or a "first plan of action" in your life right now? Why do you think this is true?

3. Describe a personal experience where God answered your specific prayer *for* your child. How did this change you?

4. Have you made it a practice to regularly pray *with* your children? If so, how has this been a meaningful experience for you and your child?

5. Looking ahead three generations, imagine what your grandchildren and great-grandchildren might face in their cultures. List three things that you can begin praying for them now.

Epilogue

Try to imagine the troubling dream that I had a few nights ago. Three generations of children have been born since that first long night I stayed up rocking Blake. Once again, our immediate family is together, since all of our children have grown old and have joined us to be with the Lord. There are quite a few other relatives we are looking after as well. Five of our seven grandchildren are still living, but some are getting up in age now. Between them—Caleb, George, Sarah, Beth, Alex, Samantha, and Joel Jr.—have had eight granddaughters of their own. Picture the family reunion we could have! It may be coming sooner than we expected. So much has changed since the new millennium came in over a century ago. Many predicted the downward spiral that followed the heralded "new age." We couldn't believe that one generation could degenerate so quickly. As adults, our own children were ostracized and lost many of their rights because of their "intolerant" faith. Two of our grandchildren were killed while serving as missionaries to Europe—now it is against the law to be a Christian on five continents. The others have suffered intense persecution. Christians are not allowed to bear male children in the new one-world government called the United Planetary Alliance. Now there has been an initiative to selectively eliminate "planetary citizens" older than age seventy. Looking back, I am grateful for the generation in which I was born. I'm afraid that my generation contributed greatly to the troubling events of late. We took our religious liberties—and the spiritual training of our children so for granted in the twentieth century.

But there's no more time or reason to dwell on the past now. We have been discussing these events in great length with Jesus. He has assured us that all of earth's times are in His control. If only we could communicate our hopeful expectation to our descendants! Already, there is a vast group of worshipers waiting with us to inhabit the wonderful kingdom that God is preparing. Uncounted millions from every nation and tribe are watching for the completion of the final chapter, so that the new heaven and earth can commence in great celebration. I see now that three of our great-great-granddaughters have joined together in prayer for their parents. I can't wait to see them and tell them how many times we prayed for the three generations following ours. God has been faithful to preserve the heritage our own grandparents began. But for now, I will sit quietly with my children until the others arrive and the night becomes day.

> Therefore, since we are surrounded by such a great cloud of witnesses, let us throw off everything that hinders and the sin that so easily entangles, and let us run with perseverance the race marked out for us. Let us fix our eyes on Jesus, the author and perfecter of our faith, who for the joy set before him endured the cross, scorning its shame, and sat down at the right hand of the throne of God. Consider Him who endured such opposition from sinful men, so that you will not grow weary and lose heart. (Heb. 12:1–3 NIV)

Appendices

CHARACTER BLUEPRINT

CHARACTER BUILDING BLUEPRINT

Appendix B-1

SAMPLE TRAINING PROCESS
STRATEGY FOR YOUR CHILD'S CHARACTER DEVELOPMENT
CHARACTER QUALITY: SELF-CONTROL

Training Ground: Competitive Athletics
Behavior Goal: Good Sportsmanship

Guidelines	Boundaries
1. Congratulate the winner.	1. Keep your temper.
2. Encourage the loser.	2. Do not brag.

Training Ground: Dinner Table
Behavior Goal: Good Manners

Guidelines	Boundaries
1. Eat what is on your plate.	1. Do not complain.
2. Chew one bite at a time.	2. Do not talk with food in your mouth.

Training Ground: Use of the Tongue
Behavior Goal: Edifying Speech

Guidelines	Boundaries
1. Always tell the truth.	1. Do not exaggerate or make things up.
2. Always be an encourager.	2. Do not tear someone down with your words.
3. Learn to be a good listener.	3. Do not always talk about yourself.

Appendix B-2

TRAINING PROCESS

STRATEGY FOR YOUR CHILD'S CHARACTER DEVELOPMENT

Character Quality:
Category: _____

Training Ground: _____
Behavior Goal: _____

<u>Guidelines</u>   <u>Boundaries</u>

1.   1.

2.   2.

3.   3.

4.   4.

(This page may be reproduced.)

Appendix C
Age-Appropriate Behavior Goals

0 to 7 Months
1. Sleep through the night
2. Develop regular schedule

8 to 14 Months
1. No crying at nap and bedtime
2. Respond to "no, no"

15 to 24 Months
1. Eye contact when parent is talking
2. Obey and yield the first time
3. Stay in the high chair
4. Say "please" and "thank you" and "yes"
5. Simple self-help: bring shoes, books, diapers
6. Eating manners: eat what is given, keep food at the table
7. Eating places: in the kitchen vs. around the house
8. Feet off the furniture/respect for home
9. Gentleness with others (no hitting, kicking, or biting)
10. Gentleness with objects (care for toys, etc.)
11. Helping others (sponge spills, pick up, etc.)
12. Prayer behavior (head bowed, quiet, etc.)

2 to 3 Years
1. Toilet training/self-help
2. Eating good foods
3. Using kind words/nice voice
4. Inside voice vs. outside voice
5. Inside play vs. outside play

6. Sharing with others, settling disputes
7. Tantrums don't work!
8. Begin dressing skills
9. Put away (cups, dirty clothes, toys)
10. Color on paper (vs. walls, floors)
11. Help clean up messes as much as possible
12. Help with family jobs (bed, table setting, yard)

4 to 8 Years

1. Obey and yield with a good attitude
2. Expand manners training (adults, table)
3. Public behavior (stores, restaurants, church)
4. Safety rules: home, yard, public, strangers, abuse
5. Kind words: consider feelings, tattling vs. telling
6. Kind actions: helping, siblings, including others
7. Following rules/asking permission (school, games)
8. Sportsmanship (winning and losing)
9. Respect for adults
10. Character traits: Source is God
11. Responsibility (self, home, school, losing things)
12. Money: saving, spending, giving
13. Reverence for God/church behavior
14. Accountability for behavior (confession, apology)
15. Constructive vs. destructive, completing a task

9 to 12 Years

1. More independence and responsibility
2. Principles behind rules
3. Expansion of manners (invitations, introductions)
4. Worship, prayer, and devotions
5. Self-discipline: body, soul, spirit
6. Character building: (sexuality added)
7. Moral development: preparing for adolescence
8. Choosing books, television, media, toys

9. Healthy friendships/being a good friend
10. Benefits of hard work
11. Sportsmanship (expanded)
12. Serving others (expanded)
13. Appropriate words to speak
14. Sibling respect and support
15. Respect for all authority figures

Goal Setting
1. Which of these goals would be appropriate for you to train at this time?

2. Are your goals balanced between respect and responsibility?

3. Are there other goals that you would add for your child's age level?

4. If your children are older, do you need to go back and retrain for any goals from an earlier age level?

Appendix D

Age-Appropriate Strategies and Tools for Discipline

0 to 7 Months
1. No direct punishment, regardless of behavior
2. Hold, love, use soothing voice
3. Feed, change, bathe, clothe
4. Provide security, affection, warmth

TOOLS: Affirm, praise

8 to 14 Months
1. First tests of authority/minor confrontations
2. Distract and divert with alternatives
3. Use persistence, not punishment
4. Don't be afraid of tears

TOOLS: Affirm, praise, reward, logical consequences, model, command, physical assistance

15 to 24 Months
1. Prepare for negativism, conflict and defiance of those who vote "no"
2. First direct punishment for willful disobedience
3. Train to obey and yield to parental leadership
4. Discern between willful disobedience and childish irresponsibility

TOOLS: Affirm, praise, reward, spank (infrequently), natural and logical consequences, explain, command, warn, ignore, physical assistance

2 to 3 Years
1. Keep sense of humor about those who "spill things, destroy things, fall off things, flush things, kill things, and get into things"
2. Win the battle for authority now, or pay later!

TOOLS: Affirm, praise, reward, spank (when needed), consequences, explain, command, warn (1-2-3), ignore, physical assistance, add time-out/isolation by age 3

4 to 8 Years
1. Obedience includes attitudes behind behavior
2. Direct character training from morning till night
3. Insist on obeying immediately, without complaint or question, and completely

TOOLS: Affirm, praise, reward, spank, consequences, explain, command, warn (once!), model, discuss ignore, time-out/ isolation, remove special privileges

9 to 12 Years
1. General loosening of the lines of authority
2. Fewer rules, less direct discipline, more independence
3. Allow more decisions about daily living
4. Relatively infrequent physical punishment

TOOLS: Affirm, praise, reward, consequences, explain, discuss, remove special privileges, spank (not often)

Appendix E

DISCIPLINE STRATEGY WORKSHEET

On a separate sheet of paper, use the following strategy to systematically work through a discipline issue with your child.

> "But if any of you [parents] lacks wisdom, let him ask of God, who gives to all men generously and without reproach, and it will be given to him." (James 1:5 NASB)

1. Describe the problem or challenge in detail. My child . . .

2. This issue concerns (list all that apply):

Respect	Immediate obedience
Responsibility	Respectful obedience
Action	Complete Obedience
Attitude	
Other . . .	

3. The child's intent seems to be . . .

4. The instruction I have given is . . .

5. The correction I have given is . . .

6. I am trying to train my child to (put in positive terms) . . .

7. The character quality I am focusing on is . . .

(This page may be reproduced.)

Appendix F

DAILY PRAYER PETITIONS

1. **Angels' protection.** "For He will command His angels concerning you to guard you in all your ways." (Psalm 91:11)
2. **A genuine conversion.** ". . . from infancy you have known the holy Scriptures, which are able to make you wise for salvation through faith in Christ Jesus." (2 Timothy 3:15)
3. **A sense of destiny.** "'For I know the plans I have for you,' declares the Lord, 'plans to prosper you and not to harm you, plans to give you hope and a future.'" (Jeremiah 29:11)
4. **Grow in faith.** "Yet he [Abraham] did not waver through unbelief regarding the promise of God, but was strengthened in his faith and gave glory to God, being fully persuaded that God had power to do what He had promised." (Romans 4:20–21)
5. **Submission to God.** "Therefore, I urge you, brothers, in view of God's mercy, to offer your bodies as living sacrifices, holy and pleasing to God this is your spiritual act of worship." (Romans 12:1)
6. **Power over sin.** ". . . We died to sin; how can we live in it any longer? . . . For sin shall no longer be your master, because you are not under law, but under grace." (Romans 6:2, 14)
7. **Please God in every way.** "And we pray this in order that you may live a life worthy of the Lord and may please Him in every way: bearing fruit in every good work. . . " (Colossians 1:10)
8. **Respect for authority.** ". . . he who rebels against the authority rebels against what God has instituted." (Romans 13:2)
9. **Teachable spirit.** "Let the wise listen and add to their learning and let the discerning get guidance . . . Listen, my son, to your

father's instruction and do not forsake your mother's teaching." (Proverbs 1:5, 8)

10. **Increasing spiritual maturity.** " . . . let us leave the elementary
teachings about Christ and go on to maturity . . . " (Hebrews
6:1)

11. **Wisdom.** "Choose my instruction instead of silver, knowledge
rather than choice gold, for wisdom is more precious than
rubies, and nothing you desire can compare with her."
(Proverbs 8:10–11)

12. **Discerning truth from error.** "So give your servant a discerning heart . . . to distinguish between right and wrong." (1
Kings 3:9)

13. **Integrity.** " . . . we have conducted ourselves in the world, and
especially in our relations with you, in the holiness and sin-
cerity that are from God . . ." (2 Corinthians 1:12)

14. **Moral purity.** "Flee from sexual immorality . . . Do you not
know that your body is a temple of the Holy Spirit . . . ?" (1
Corinthians 6:18–19)

15. **Courage.** " . . . Be strong and courageous. Do not be terrified;
do not be discouraged, for the Lord your God will be with you
wherever you go." (Joshua 1:9)

16. **Perseverance.** " . . . Stand firm. Let nothing move you. Always
give yourselves fully to the work of the Lord, because you
know that your labor in the Lord is not in vain."(1 Corinthians
15:58)

17. **Self-Discipline.** " . . .discipline yourself for the purpose of
godliness; for bodily discipline is only of little profit, but godliness is profitable for all things, since it holds promise for the
present life to come." (1 Timothy 4: 7, 8)

18. **Usefulness to God.** " . . . make every effort to add to your faith
goodness; and to goodness, knowledge; and to knowledge, self-
control; and to self-control, perseverance; and to perseverance, godliness; and to godliness, brotherly kindness; and to

brotherly kindness, love. For if you possess these qualities in increasing measure, they will keep you from being ineffective and unproductive in your knowledge of our Lord Jesus Christ." (2 Peter 1:5–8)

19. **A sensitive heart.** "Therefore, as God's chosen people, holy and dearly loved, clothe yourselves with compassion, kindness, humility, gentleness and patience." (Colossians 3:12)

20. **A cheerful heart.** "A cheerful heart is good medicine . . . " (Proverbs 17:22a)

21. **A serving heart.** "Your attitude should be the same as that of Christ Jesus: Who . . . made Himself nothing, taking the very nature of a servant . . ." (Philippians 2: 5–7)

22. **A grateful heart.** "Be glad in the Lord, you righteous ones; And give thanks to His holy name." (Psalm 97:12 NASB)

23. **Perspective on possessions.** "But godliness with contentment is great gain. For we brought nothing into the world, and we can take nothing out of it. But if we have food and clothing, we will be content with that." (1 Timothy 6:6–8)

24. **Pursuit of excellence.** "Whatever you do, work at it with all your heart, as working for the Lord, not for men." (Colossians 3:23)

25. **Protection from the evil one.** "My prayer is not that You take them out of the world but that You protect them from the evil one." (John 17:15)

26. **Overcome Satan's temptations.** "Because he himself suffered when he was tempted, he is able to help those who are being tempted." (Hebrews 2:18)

27. **Avoid negative influences.** "My son, if sinners entice you, do not give in to them . . . do not set foot on their paths." (Proverbs 1:10, 15)

28. **Godly friends.** "Then Daniel returned to his house and explained the matter to his friends . . . He urged them to plead for mercy from the God of heaven . . . Then Nebuchadnezzar

said, 'Praise be to the God of Shadrach, Meshach, and Abednego, who . . . trusted in Him . . . and were willing to give up their lives rather than serve or worship any god except their own God.'" (Daniel 2:17–18; 3:28)

29. **Godly life partner.** "Do not be bound together with unbelievers; for what partnership have righteousness and lawlessness, or what fellowship has light with darkness?" (2 Corinthians 6:14 NASB)

30. **A consistent walk.** "Blessed is the man who does not walk in the counsel of the wicked or stand in the way of the sinners or sit in the seat of the mockers. But his delight is in the law of the Lord, and on His law he meditates day and night. He is like a tree planted by streams of water, which yields its fruit in season and whose leaf does not wither . . ." (Psalm 1:1–3)

31. **Long, prosperous life.** "My son, do not forget my teaching, but keep my commands in your heart, for they will prolong your life many years and bring you prosperity." (Proverbs 3:1–2)

Appendix G

Scripture Memory from A to Z

A For all have sinned and fall short of the glory of God. (Romans 3:23)

B Believe in the Lord Jesus, and you will be saved. (Acts 16:31)

C Children, obey your parents in the Lord, for this is right. (Ephesians 6:1)

D Turn from evil and do good. (Psalm 34:14 NKJV)

E Even a child is known by his actions. (Proverbs 20:11)

F Fear not for I am with you. (Isaiah 43:5 NKJV)

G God is love. (1 John 4:8)

H Honor your father and your mother. (Exodus 20:12)

I I am the vine; you are the branches. (John 15:5)

J Jesus said, "I am the way and the truth and the life. No man comes to the Father, but by me." (John 14:6)

K Keep your tongue from evil. (Psalm 34:13)

L Look unto me and be ye saved. (Isaiah 45:22)

M Marvel not. You must be born again. (John 3:7)

N No one can serve two masters. (Matthew 6:24)

O Oh give thanks to the Lord for He is good. (Psalm:118:1)

P Praise the Lord! (Psalm 147:1)

Q Quench not the spirit. (1 Thessalonians 5:19)

R Remember the Sabbath day to keep it holy. (Exodus 20:8)

S Seek ye first the kingdom of God. (Matthew 6:33)

T Thou God seest me. (Genesis 16:13)

U Unto us a child is born. (Isaiah 9:6 NKJV)

V Verily, verily I say to you, whatsoever you shall ask the Father in my name He will give it to you. (John 16:23)

W Wait on the Lord and keep His way holy. (Psalm 37:34)

X   Exceeding great and precious promises are given to us. (2 Peter 1:4 NKJV)

Y   You are the light of the world. (Matthew 5:14)

Z   Zion heard and was glad. (Psalm 97:8)

Notes

Chapter One

1. "Kids Who Kill: When Boys Go Bad," *Time*, 6 July 1998, 58.
2. Josh McDowell and Bob Hostetler, *Right from Wrong* (Dallas: Word, 1994), 254–63.
3. Barnes and Noble.com, Reviews and Commentary reviewing, *Maybe One: A Personal and Environmental Argument for Single-Child Families* by Bill McKibben, (New York: Simon and Schuster, 1998).
4. David Elkind, *The Hurried Child: Growing Up Too Fast, Too Soon* (Reading, MA: Addison-Wesley, 1988), xii–xiii.
5. Elmer L. Towns, *How to Reach the Baby Boomer: Ministering to the 21st Century Church* (Lynchburg, VA: Church Growth Institute, 1990).
6. Adapted from James Dobson, *Hide Or Seek* (Old Tappan, NJ: Fleming H. Revell, 1974).

Chapter Two

1. Bobby Moore, "Any Old Port in a Storm," *First Baptist Informer* (Mineral Wells, TX: First Baptist Church, May 13, 1981).
2. *Focus on the Family* (October 1986).
3. Leigh Montville, "Nobody Saw It Coming," *Sports Illustrated*, 17 August 1998, 36–43.
4. Dale Hanson Bourke, "Motherhood, It will change your life," *Guideposts*, May 1990. Excerpted from *Everyday Miracles: Holy Moments in a Mother's Day* by Dale Hanson Bourke, (Irving, Texas: Word, 1989).

Chapter Three
1. Robert Wolgemuth, at a Christian Businessmen's Luncheon, Nashville, TN, Fall 1993.
2. Lisa Easterwood, Christmas newsletter, 1990, by permission.
3. Steve Farrar, *Point Man* (Portland, OR: Multnomah Press, 1990), 81–82.

Chapter Four
1. Catherine Marshall Le Sourd, *Something More* (New York, NY: Avon Books, 1974), 59.
2. Kevin Lehman and Randy Carlson, *Unlocking the Secrets of Your Childhood Memories* (Nashville, TN: Thomas Nelson, 1989), 188.
3. Steve Farrar, *Point Man* (Portland, OR: Multnomah Press, 1990), 26.
4. *Sermons Illustrated* (Holland, OH: Jeff and Pam Carroll, May 1989).
5. Neil T. Anderson, *The Bondage Breaker* (Eugene, OR: Harvest House, 1990), 23.
6. Lynda Hunter, *Parenting On Your Own* (Grand Rapids, MI: Zondervan, 1997).
7. Lehman and Carlson, *Unlocking the Secrets of Your Childhood Memories*, 20.

Chapter Five
1. Max Lucado. *No Wonder They Call Him Savior,* (Eugene, OR: Multnomah, 1986), 31–32.
2. Individuals With Disabilities Education Act (IDEA), 1990, P.L. 99–457, Part H Program (Early Intervention Program for Infants and Toddlers with Disabilities.)

Chapter Six
1. Tim Hansel's letter to Charles Swindoll cited in *Sermons Illustrated* (Holland, OH: Jeff and Pam Carroll, 1990).

2. Kent and Barbara Hughes, *Liberating Ministry from the Success Syndrome* (Wheaton, IL: Tyndale House, 1988), 71.

Chapter Seven

1. Josh McDowell and Bob Hostetler, *Right from Wrong* (Dallas, TX: Word, 1994), 81.
2. Student Discipleship Ministries, *My Quiet Time*, Daily Devotional Guides, Series J, (Ft. Worth, Texas, Student Discipleship Ministries, 1996), 18.

Chapter Eight

1. Sharon Begley, "Do Parents Matter? The Parent Trap," *Newsweek*, 7 September 1998, 52–59.
2. Stanton L. Jones and Brenna B. Jones, *How and When To Tell Your Kids About Sex: A Lifelong Approach to Shaping Your Child's Sexual Character* (Colorado Springs: NavPress, 1993).
3. *Compton's Encyclopedia* (Chicago, IL: University of Chicago, 1989 ed.), vol. 23, 16.

Chapter Nine

1. Ann Landers, cited in *Sermons Illustrated* (Holland, OH: Jeff and Pam Carroll, April 1990).
2. James Strong, S.T.D., LL.D., *Abingdon's Strong's Exhaustive Concordance of the Bible* (Nashville, TN: Abingdon Press, 1890).
3. Tim Kimmel, *Legacy of Love* (Portland, OR: Multnomah Press, 1989), 108.
4. James Dobson, *Focus on the Family* radio program.
5. James P. Lenfestey, "Catch of a Lifetime," *Minneapolis Star Tribune*, 15 May 1988.
6. Billy Beacham, *Growing in Godliness Leader's Guide* (Fort Worth, TX: Student Discipleship Ministries, 1986), 13–14.

Chapter Ten

1. Ann Landers, cited in *Sermons Illustrated* (Holland, OH: Jeff and Pam Carroll, May 1990).
2. Lynda Hunter, *Parenting on Your Own* (Grand Rapids, MI: Zondervan, 1997).
3. Irene Endicott, *Grandparenting by Grace* (Nashville, TN: Broadman & Holman, 1994).
4. Steve Farrar, *Point Man* (Portland, OR: Multnomah, 1990), 259–260.
5. Student Discipleship Ministries, *True Test* (Fort Worth, TX: SDM, 1989), 52–53.

Chapter Eleven

1. *Focus on the Family* magazine, October 1986.
2. Turning Point, *Divine Appointments* (Ft. Worth, Texas, Student Discipleship Ministries, 1994), 23.
3. Claudia Arp, *MOMS* video series.
4. "For Our Teenagers," *Pulpit Helps*, January 1992, 20.

Chapter Twelve

1. Steve Farrar, Adapted from an illustration used at the Family Life Conference, Memphis, TN, 1987.
2. Gary Smalley, *The Key to Your Child's Heart* (Waco, TX: Word, 1984), 20, 41–42.
3. James Dobson, *Parenting Isn't for Cowards* (Waco, TX: Word, 1987), 36–50.
4. Stanley Turecki, *The Difficult Child.*
5. Student Discipleship Ministries, *My Quiet Time,* Daily Devotional Guides, Series D, (Ft. Worth, Texas, Student Discipleship Ministries, 1996), 15.

Chapter Thirteen

1. Compiled by Stuart Hampel and Eric Marshall, *Children's*

Letters to God: The New Collection (New York, NY: Workman Publishing, 1991), 8, 37, 83, 89.

2. *Sermons Illustrated* (Holland, OH: Jeff and Pam Carroll, May 1990).

3. Will Allen Dromgoole, "The Bridge Builder," in *The Book of Virtues* (New York, NY: Simon & Schuster, 1993), 223.

Chapter Fourteen

1. Christine Wicker, "Steadfast Faith Comforts Family," *Dallas Morning News*, 15 December 1996, 1, 32A.

Chapter Fifteen

1. Bill Gillham, adapted from What God *Wishes Christians Knew about Christianity* (Harvest House, 1998), 263.

2. Charles Swindoll, *You and Your Child* (Nashville, TN: Thomas Nelson, Bantam ed., 1980), 8.

3. Turning Point, *Divine Appointments* (Ft. Worth, TX, Student Discipleship Ministries, 1994), 6.

4. Bernard L. Brown, Jr., quoted in "Who Does What When?," *Bits and Pieces*, 16 September 1993, 22–24.

5. Michael C. Catt, "From the Cluttered Desk," newsletter of Sherwood Church, vol. 44, ed. 35, August 30, 1998.

6. Billy Beacham, George Guthrie and Student Discipleship Ministries Staff, *Everyone, Everywhere* (Ft. Worth, TX: Student Discipleship Ministries, 1990), 25–26.

Chapter Sixteen

1. David and Elaine Atchison, *Shaping the Next Generation Leader's Guide* (Ft. Worth, TX: Turning Point, 1992), 118–819.

2. IEA Staff and First Baptist, Burleson, Texas, Youth Ministries, *My Quiet Time* (Ft. Worth, TX: International Evangelism Association, 1984).

3. Turning Point, *Divine Appointments* (Ft. Worth, Texas, Student Discipleship Ministries, 1994), 9.

4. Patrick Morley, *Man in the Mirror* (Nashville, TN: Wolgemuth and Hyatt, 1989), 96.

5. *Sermons Illustrated* (Holland, OH: Jeff and Pam Carroll, June 1990).

6. Turning Point, *Divine Appointments* (Ft. Worth, Texas, Student Discipleship Ministries, 1994), 51.

7. Steve Farrar, *Point Man* (Portland, OR: Multnomah Press, 1990), 154.

About the Authors

David Atchison spent over a decade developing and operating several corporations in the field of commercial real estate. Elaine Atchison is trained as a speech-language pathologist, specializing in infant and early language development. The culmination of many years of speaking, teaching, and writing for youth and adults was the founding of a teaching and writing ministry known as Disciple's Call. David and Elaine have a passion for equipping men and women to discover their unique calling and developing a lifestyle of disciplemaking. They are also the authors of a devotional guide called *Divine Appointments* and a video-driven interactive study course called *Shaping the Next Generation*. Their primary ministry continues to be parenting three teenaged children in Franklin, Tennessee.

They may be contacted by writing or calling:
Disciple's Call
P.O. Box 680338
Franklin, TN 37068
615-791-9782